TEXAS HIG

FOOT

MORE THA

BY JOE NIC

H SCHOOL

BALL

THE GAME

K PATOSKI

Buckaroo Stadium At Breckenri[dge]
during The Waco Game
Breck. 14   Waco
P.E. Shotwell Bucks Coach.
Basil Clemons
1929

ISBN 978-0-292-73887-4 (paperback)
ISBN 978-0-292-73886-7 (cloth)
1. Football—Texas—History. 2. Football—Texas—Memorabilia 3. School
sports—Texas—History
I. Patoski, Joe Nick, 1951-

Distributed by The University of Texas Press
2100 Comal Street
Austin, Texas 78722

This publication accompanies the exhibition Texas High School Football:
More Than The Game presented at The Bob Bullock Texas State History
Museum from July 30, 2011 to January 22, 2012.

Cover
Ed Bernet, Highland Park High School, Dallas, Texas, 1950, Photograph by
Laughead Studio, courtesy of Texas High School Football Hall of Fame, Waco

Inside front cover
Mustang Bowl, Sweetwater, Texas, Photograph by Jeff Wilson

Page 4
Buckaroo Stadium, Breckenridge, Texas, 1929, Courtesy Basil Clemons
Photograph Collection, Special Collections, The University of Texas at
Arlington Library

Back Cover
Big Sandy Wildcats Take the Field, 1976, photograph by Geoff Winningham,
Smithsonian American Art Museum, Transfer from The National Endowment
for the Arts

San Antonio Churchill HS helmet, Courtesy Texas High School Football Hall
of Fame, Waco, ca. 1980-81

Book and cover design by DJ Stout and Barrett Fry
Pentagram, Austin, Texas

INTRODUCTION

What does high school football have to do with Texas history? Quite a bit, it turns out. Over a relatively short period of time, Texas high school football has evolved into a vital nexus of every community in the state. Its impact on the greater culture is profound. In our cities, suburbs, and rural towns, the stature and reputation of a community's football team is a matter of serious business and serious braggin' rights.

The story of Texas high school football continues to unfold, because history is, in essence, an exercise in interpretation. We filter the past through the lens of the evolving present. Despite significant demographic shifts in Texas, from rural to urban to suburban, supporting the local high school football team is a rite and responsibility that endures in communities large and small, old and new. Friday night lights are an integral part of our state's identity and now define the Lone Star State throughout the world.

When the museum decided to do an exhibition on Texas high school football, our goal was to explore the bigger story behind it, not just recite facts and statistics for every player, team and division. We wanted to understand what inspires communities to support their football programs with such fervor, sometimes bordering on the outlandish. We wanted to look at every facet of Texas high school football, from booster clubs to homecoming mums, and discover what makes it "more than the game."

Texas is one of the most diverse states in the nation. High school football helps to transcend this diversity by creating common aspirations and a communal identity. Few things in Texas connect individuals and create community more than supporting the local high school football team.

Passions run deep for Texas high school football and this was apparent from the very first meeting of the exhibit's Advisory Committee, made up of sports scholars, museum curators, football aficionados and, of course, coaches. We are grateful for the input and ongoing support of Coach Eddie Joseph, former director of the Texas High School Coaches Association, as well as Jay Black and Paige Davis from the Texas Sports Hall of Fame. Joe Lee Smith helped us make critical connections. Granger Huntress and Leman Saunders introduced us to everything Six Man football has to offer.

Several individuals and organizations supported our research, including Mark Cousins, Athletic Director at the University Interscholastic League, D. W. Rutledge, Executive Director at the Texas High School Coaches Association, Robert Brown, current Board Chair for the Prairie View Interscholastic League Coaches Association, Bill Minter of the Abilene Preservation League, and Lonn Taylor.

Joe Nick Patoski, the exhibit's guest curator, burned through his allotted travel allowance twice over and continued on to cover more miles and attend more games on his own dime. The relationships he developed were crucial to this exhibit, resulting in over 100 lenders of 200+ artifacts, the largest special exhibit in the Museum's history. We thank him for his insightful essay and epic historical timeline of Texas high school football.

Bill Kennedy, Professor of Photocommunications at St. Edwards University, enlisted eight of his students to photograph football rituals throughout the state—more than forty of these images are featured in the exhibition. Bill's own masterful Texas high school football photographs are featured in a rotating series of solo photography shows within the Museum's exhibit, along with the iconic work of photographers Nancy Newberry, Jeff Wilson, Laura Wilson, and Geoff Winningham.

Castleview Productions, the media producer for the exhibit, went well beyond their contracted scope of work to produce a series of compelling oral histories and a comprehensive video production worthy of national awards. Jay B Sauceda did a superb job of photographing the artifacts for the exhibition catalogue. Museum interns Corrie Moak, Joel Dishman, and Jordan Lewis contacted nearly every school district in the state, fact checking school histories and identifying mascots and team records.

This exhibit and catalogue could not have been accomplished without the dedicated efforts of the Museum staff, especially Exhibits Planner Tom Wancho, Exhibit Content Coordinator Kathryn Siefker, and Registrar Kathleen Stiefel. Toni Beldock, Head of Exhibits, and her expert crew have done an extraordinary job in producing a compelling exhibition.

We are grateful for the financial support of The Reilly Family Foundation, The Discovery Fund, Dodge Jones Foundation, Humanities Texas, Abilene Sports Alliance, Stan Lambert, Julie and Mike Denny, and Johan Green. In-kind support provided to this exhibit by All-Star Inflatables, AstroTurf, and Mission Restaurant Supply is very much appreciated. Special thanks to Christina Patoski who made this catalogue a reality.

DAVID DENNEY
Director of Public Programming
The Bob Bullock Texas State History Museum
Austin, Texas

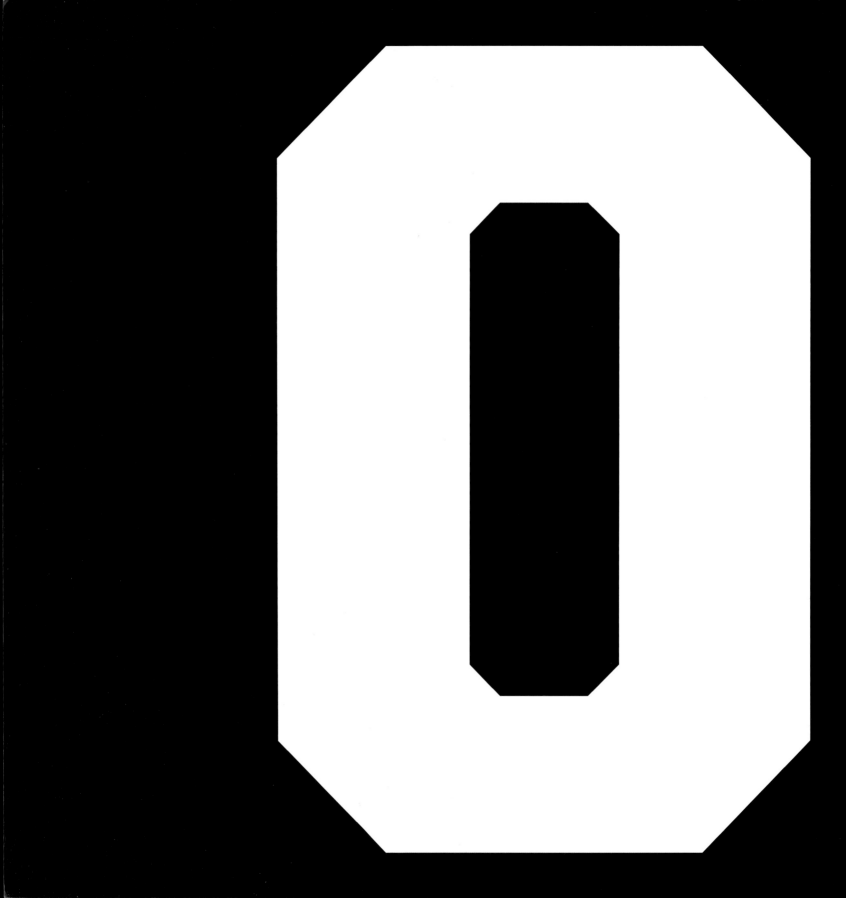

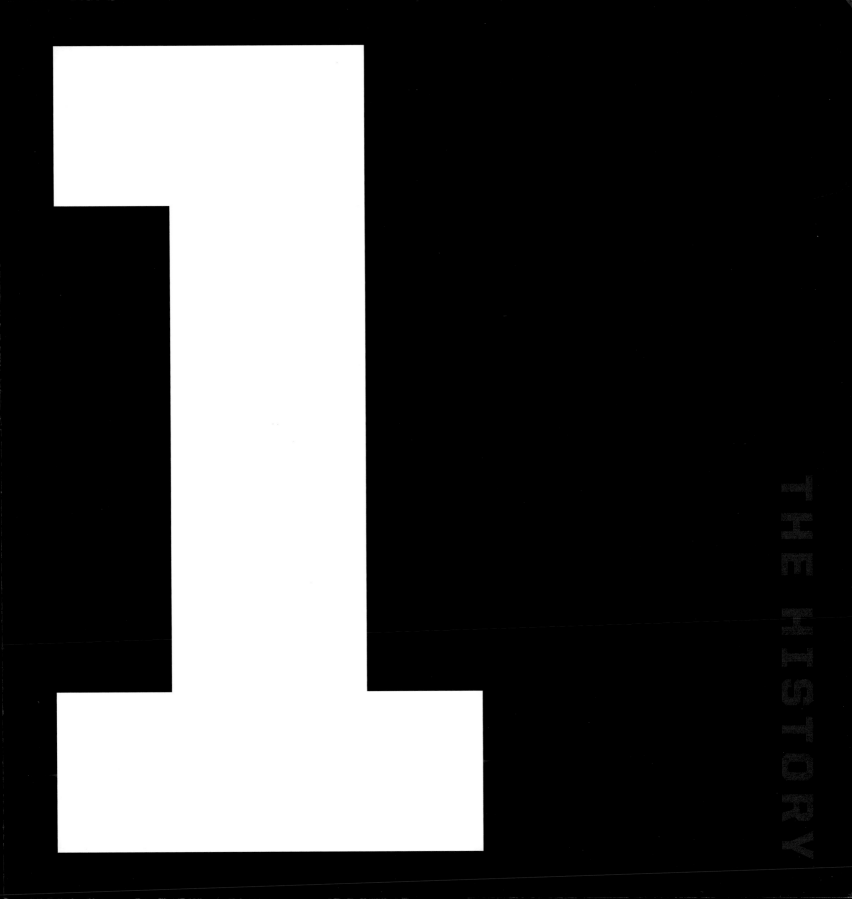

Big Sandy Wildcats Take the Field *1976, photograph by Geoff Winningham, Smithsonian American Art Museum, Transfer from The National Endowment for the Arts*

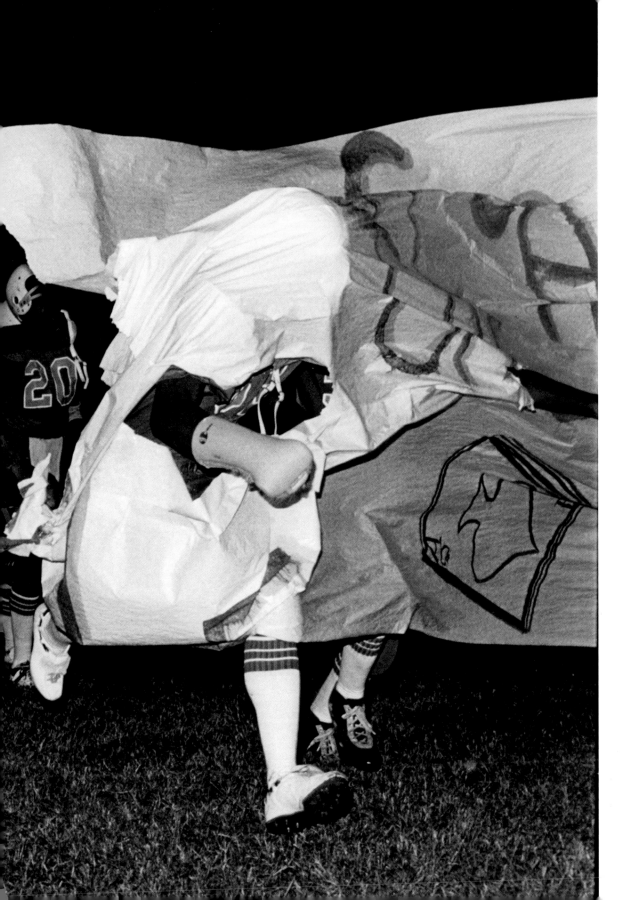

TEXAS HIGH SCHOOL FOOTBALL
MORE THAN THE GAME

Over the past two seasons, I have traveled thousands of miles across Texas to witness Texas high school football. I have seen the game played on every level and under every condition imaginable, from tiny schools with Six Man teams played in aged stadiums where every fan's voice can be heard, to large schools with college-level programs played in modern state-of-the-art facilities in front of more than 40,000 fans. My travels took me from Brownsville to Canadian and from El Paso to Orange. It didn't matter whether the game was played in a torrid heat wave, in sleet and snow at the height of a blue norther, in a pounding rainstorm accompanied by hurricane-strength winds, in a climate-controlled indoor stadium, or under a brilliant star-lit sky on a perfect October evening - the conclusion was inevitably the same: no one does high school football like Texans do.

Football may be the American game, played by all ages and on all levels of competency, but nowhere else does it excite passions, instill pride, and generate the intensity it does in Texas on the high school level. Over 100,000 high school boys (and a few girls) participate in the sport, supported by their coaches and trainers, and the hundreds of thousands of students who march in the band, lead cheers, perform dance and drill routines, dress up as mascots, or simply sit in the stands, along with their families, friends, relatives, teachers, and plain old fans. Ask any of them and they'll tell you: Texas high school football is more than just the game.

From late August into December, lights illuminate the skies across Texas every Friday night. Each point of light marks the spot where Texas high school football is being played—in big cities, small towns, isolated rural outposts, and brand new suburbs in every nook and cranny of the state. Like cattle, horses, and the weather, high school football is that rare subject that transcends language, economic status, ethnicity, faith, and geographic differences to bring folks together. It is a game, but it is also a participatory ritual celebrating team, school, and community.

HISTORY High school football in Texas has a rich, storied past that covers more than twelve decades, beginning with the first high school team that represented Ball High School in Galveston in 1892. Since then, the game and its participants have evolved to inform its current popularity and role in modern Texas culture. Its history is told by schools such as Ball High, Waco High, the Masonic Home High, Cleburne High, Breckenridge High, Brownwood High, Daingerfield High, LaMarque High, and Katy High; players such as

Ballinger Blocking Board in action *Courtesy Texas High School Football Hall of Fame, Waco, ca. 1936*

Boody Johnson, Sammy Baugh, Y. A. Tittle, Tom Landry, Earl Campbell, Forrest Gregg, John Hardy, Ty and Koy Detmer, Willie Mack Garza, Robert Strait, and Lovie Smith; and coaches such as Paul Tyson, Blair Cherry, Luther Booker, E. C. Lerma, Gordon Wood, Emory Bellard, and G. A. Moore. Each and every person to ever step on a football field knows the special feeling: whether they excelled or didn't even play, the game, in some form or fashion, helped shape and define their lives.

UIL In 1910, the Interscholastic Athletics Association was created through the University of Texas Extension Service to govern athletics in Texas public schools. The non-profit organization joined with the Debating League of Texas in 1913 to form the University Interscholastic League (UIL) for governing academics, music, and athletic contests. The UIL enforced rules and regulations for football, which at the time was rife with cheating, outlaw behavior, and gambling. The playoff system leading to the UIL state championship was developed by director Roy Bedichek. Schools were split into two conferences, A and B, determined by student body size and geography. Each B conference region of the state held its own championship. At the end of the season, the best A conference teams in North Texas and South Texas squared off. The first official championship game was played at Clark Field on the University of Texas campus in December 1920, with Heights High School of Houston tying Cleburne High School 0-0.

PVIL Prior to the U.S. Supreme Court's landmark 1954 *Brown v. Board of Education* decision, segregation laws in Texas mandated separate schools for African Americans and in some areas for Mexican Americans. In keeping with this policy, the University Interscholastic League limited membership to "white" public schools. Still, black teams were common throughout Texas, and in 1920 the Texas Interscholastic League of Colored Schools formed, evolving into the Prairie View Interscholastic League (PVIL) under the authority of Prairie View A&M. PVIL was the governing body for athletics, typing, public speaking, music, and extemporaneous speaking contests. Since laws separating races in schools were done away with, the PVIL has been forgotten by the general public. But accomplishments by "colored" school athletes remain undisputed, despite having to play with hand-me-down equipment and uniforms on Thursdays and Saturdays because fields were reserved for white schools on Fridays. The Lincoln High Bumble Bees of Port Arthur, for example, sent thirteen football players to the professional ranks. If not for the PVIL, athletes such as Mean Joe Greene (Temple Dunbar), Ernie Banks (Dallas Booker T. Washing-

ton), and Abner Haynes (Dallas Lincoln) would not have achieved national recognition.

RIVALRIES The rivalry game is the game upon which the season is measured, regardless of how many wins or losses either school has. It is the game that matters most and generates the greatest intensity. Geography, shared boundaries, and history create the kind of rivalries where tempers flare on and off the field, pranks are played, players hit harder, and scores are settled for the year on the field and in the stands. Some rivalries are immediate, such as when a new school is spun from an existing school. Other rivalries take decades to develop. Redistricting, school growth, and consolidation end or threaten many rivalries, such as the Chili Bowl in San Antonio between Lanier and Fox Tech, which ended a 67-year run when Fox Tech dropped football, or when Beaumont Hebert and Beaumont Charlton-Pollard were consolidated into Ozen High.

One of the oldest rivalries in Texas is the Guadalupe River Shootout between Seguin and New Braunfels on which mayors have bet pecans for sausage for the last 96 years. The Battle of the Rice Prairie between the El Campo Ricebirds and the Bay City Black Cats is perhaps the oldest rivalry, having started in 1911. A rivalry with a quirky twist is The Border Battle or The State Line Game in Texarkana when the Texas High Tigers play the Arkansas Razorbacks. The teams have fought for the Battle Axe since 1912. The game begins with a bacon fry pep rally on the Texas side.

RITUALS For months leading up to the start of school, students participating in every facet of the fall Friday night pageant invest hundreds of hours of preparation, dedicating themselves to be the best they can be. Football players, band members, cheerleaders, dancers, mascots, boosters, and everyone involved in Friday night football sacrifices every moment of their time to prepare for the upcoming season by the time kickoff rolls around.

Homecoming is the biggest, richest tradition of Texas high school football, the pinnacle of the game's pageantry, and its most popular rite of passage. It originally gained popularity as an annual event to welcome back alumni on the same day as a home football game, as was the case with the first collegiate homecoming at Baylor University in Waco in 1909. Homecoming today can include a special pep rally, a popularity contest resulting in the coronation of a Homecoming Queen and King from the senior class during halftime, a dance after the game for students, often a parade, and the conspicuous display of elaborate mum corsages at school, at the game, and at the dance. The exchange and wearing of mums and garters between students of all classes is another element of high school football that separates Texas from everywhere else. The customized corsages consist of one or more mums decorated with pipe cleaners, ribbons, trinkets, bells, and other decorations to distinguish the person wearing them, their class, their school, and their mascot. Mums are sold in flower shops, super markets, and craft stores but many are handmade by women in the community for whom homecoming mums are a cottage industry.

Visit a high school campus on a Friday afternoon and you will hear a deafening noise coming from the gymnasium. Inside you will find the final prelude to game time—the pep rally. The pep rally is the big send off, meant to inspire, unite, motivate, and rouse both the players and their supporters before going into battle, accompanied by signs, painted faces, painted bodies, and a whole lot of spirit. The key participants in the pep rally are the cheerleaders and mascot who organize the rally and perform the cheers and skits designed to boost school spirit. They are supported by the band which provides the music to rev up the crowd. The coaches and players offer testimonials and pep talks. And underlining it all are the students who build up the enthusiasm, along with the teachers, parents, and families who show up to lend their support.

MASCOTS Texas does mascots like nowhere else. Over the past thirty years mascots have evolved from an image affixed to helmets, banners, flags, and pennants to the literal face of the school – a student performing alongside the cheerleaders in a costume, typically with an oversized head. The most common mascots of Texas high schools are Eagles, Bulldogs, Tigers, and Panthers. But the entire animal kingdom is well-represented, along with creatures both real and imaginary.

Some Texas high school mascots emphasize fighting spirits, including numerous Pirates, Buccaneers, and Raiders. Predatory mammals, reptiles and insects feared by humans are especially popular, such as the Anna and Wichita Falls Coyotes, the Progreso Red Ants, Rattlers, Lobos, Loboes, Cougars, Leopards, Longhorns, Brahmas, Steers, Hornets, Yellow Jackets, and Wildcats.

Historical references define some school mascots, thus the Boswell Pioneers, Lubbock Westerners, Plainview Plainsmen, Arlington Bowie Volunteers, Rosenberg Terry Rangers, San Antonio Roosevelt Rough Riders, Center Roughriders, and various Rebels.

The local economy inspired the Robstown Cottonpickers, the Sundown, Columbia, and White Oak Roughnecks, Brazosport Exporters, Texas City and Victoria Stingarees, Port Lavaca Calhoun Fighting Sand Crabs, Pearland Oilers, Diboll Lumberjacks, Mason Punchers, Pampa Harvesters, Lewisville Fightin' Farmers, Roscoe Plowboys, Cuero Gobblers, Hereford Whitefaces, Falfurrias Fighting Jerseys, El Paso Irvin, San Antonio Kennedy and San Antonio Judson Rockets, Wellington Sky Rockets, San Antonio Randolph Ro-Hawks, and Knippa Rockcrushers.

Domestic livestock and local wildlife are the inspiration for the San Saba Armadillos, Fredericksburg Battlin' Billies, Kerrville Tivy Fighting Antlers, White Deer and Alpine Bucks, Rocksprings Angoras, Groesbeck Goats, Port Isabel Tarpons, El Campo Ricebirds, Rotan Yellowhammers, and Nazareth Swifts.

Distinctive geographic or environmental features are behind the naming of the Floydada Whirlwinds, Memphis Cyclones, Lamesa Golden Tornadoes, Jayton Jaybirds, Amarillo Golden Sandstorm, or Sandies, Grapeland Sandies, Winters Blizzards, Frost Polar Bears, and Highlands Chinquapin Burrs.

An exceptional number of unusual and sometimes inscrutable mascots represent Texas high schools, among them the New Braunfels Unicorns, various Dragons, the Bryan St. Michael's Academy Dragonslayers, Hamlin Pied Pipers, Austin Maroons, the Itasca Wampus Cats, Van Vandals, the Trent Gorillas, Baytown Lee Ganders, Masonic Home Mighty Mites, Fort Worth Poly Parrots, Frisco Fightin' Raccoons, Grandview Zebras, the Munday Moguls, Lake Worth Bullfrogs, Springtown Fighting Porcupines, Alamo Heights and Muleshoe Mules, Mesquite Skeeters, Taylor Fighting Ducks, the Weatherford, Kress, and Killeen Kangaroos, San Antonio Central Catholic Buttons, San Antonio Lanier Voks, and the Hutto Hippos.

In recent years, the use of Indians as mascots has been criticized and discontinued by most football teams. While many teams in Texas have resisted the pressure, three schools have gone beyond the mascot to embrace their tribal identification.

West Texas High School in Stinnett was adopted by the Comanche Nation in 1989. The school displays the Tu'Wee Comanche constitution at the administration building and raises a tipi by the stadium before home games. At homecoming the coach throws a spear, igniting a "WT" metal frame.

The Port Neches-Groves Indians were inspired by local history. The town site of Port Neches was the home of the only Indian village in present day Jefferson County. The Cherokee Nation presented Port Neches-Groves High School with their official seal in 1979, giving the school the right to have its teams be called the Indians. The PN-G Stadium is called The Reservation and the school's richest traditions are tied directly to the Cherokee.

Ysleta High School in El Paso is the high school for the Tigua nation. The Indians' pregame rituals include players paying respect to the wood carving of Kawliga in the school's foyer the afternoon before a game, and a student riding a horse onto the field before home games to throw a spear into the ground of the field.

TAKING THE FIELD Few rituals can stir the soul like the anticipation of opening kickoff. The various participants enter the stadium and walk onto the field in separate parades. The sound of the marching band builds the excitement, as do the drill team captains shouting commands to keep the squad together as they enter. The growing buzz of expectation builds as the scoreboard clock ticks down to 0:00. Volunteers selling programs and boosters selling food, trinkets, and raffle tickets chime in. The echoes of welcome from the public address announcer are another signal. Then come the teams running onto the field as the band plays, the student exchange of gifts at midfield, the coin toss between team captains, the national anthem, the alma maters, the fight songs, and the first cheers of the evening. And then, with the opening kickoff, it begins.

THE FIELD The football field is traditionally a grass surface. Since the development of AstroTurf as a playing surface for the world's first domed stadium, the Houston Astrodome, in 1966. Texas high schools have increasingly embraced artificial turf made of synthetic fibers to reduce wear and tear and save on maintenance and irrigating expenses. The cost of installing artificial turf for a football field ranges from $300,000 to over $1 million.

COACHES The coach has many roles: teacher, producer, conductor, strategist, tactician, role model, salesman, and promoter. He can be a gruff drill sergeant who instills discipline. He can be a surrogate parent, as Ray Seals was to Vince Young at Madison High in Houston. He can be a motivator like Chuck Curtis, who used evangelical skills learned from the pulpit and armchair psychology to get his boys at Cleburne going. The coach teaches and guides the players, demonstrating the techniques of the game, instilling pride and developing character while organizing the team. The coach is also the face of the team and the school in the community. As such, one of the greatest roles of a coach can be to inspire humanity. In 2008, Coach Kris Hogan of Grapevine Faith Christian School challenged Coach Mark Williams of the Gainesville State School, a maximum-security facility of the Texas Youth Commission for juveniles, to a game, creating what has become an annual event, the One Heart Bowl. Students, family, and faculty from Grapevine crossed over to cheer for the Gainesville Tornadoes, showing that humanity is an important component of winning. For a coach, success is not just measured on the scoreboard. A good coach teaches social skills, decency, morality, commitment, and life's lessons in addition to Xs and Os.

The Texas High School Coaches Association organizes, advises, and lobbies for Texas high school coaches. The largest such organization in the United States, the THSCA stages an annual convention every summer with coaching clinics, panels, and a trade show that draws more than 12,000 coaches. Current president D. W. Rutledge is the winningest coach ever from the San Antonio area. Past president Eddie Joseph is the patron of one of Texas's most storied coaching families.

PLAYERS The players are the heart and soul of Texas high school football. For days, weeks, months, and years they train and practice in anticipation of walking onto the biggest stage of their lives. The thrill of taking the field to run, block, tackle, pass, catch, collide, and compete is beyond compare. Regardless of their success, individuals learn to share the joy of victory and the sorrow of defeat,

Mullin cheerleaders
Democrat, Texas, 1995
Photograph by Laura Wilson

and better understand the power that comes from working together towards the same goal as a team.

Suiting up in front of the people who know them best is an accomplishment unto itself. Growing up in Gilmer, Harold Leverett learned that once he started playing football, "everyone in town knew who I was when I walked into the barber shop." Jerry LeVias remembered hearing the big boys from Charlton-Pollard singing the team song on the bus on their way to their games and wanting to do that someday, too.

Skills or no skills, standout starter or benchwarmer, undersized underdogs like Squirt Thomas, physically-challenged boys such as Lefty Lincoln, and Can't Miss prospects like Bub Deerinwater and Joe Don Looney, it really doesn't matter. For many, playing high school football is a high point of their lives. Nothing else comes close.

OFFICIALS Officials enforce the rules of football, calling penalties when the rules are broken and

to dance, jump, kick, and perform gymnastic stunts individually and with partners. Cheerleaders often participate in local, regional, and national cheerleading competitions organized by several organizations, including the Texas-based National Cheerleaders Association and the Universal Cheerleaders Association.

High school cheerleading grew out of pep squads in the 1920s and has evolved from a male-dominated activity to mixed-partners to predominantly female squads. Contemporary cheerleading is divided into two schools—those who lead cheers and those who specialize in stunts and gymnastics and compete in contests after football season.

Like other aspects of Friday night football, Texas is recognized as the wellspring of high school cheerleading. Lawrence Herkimer is known as the Mr. Cheerleader USA. He grew up in Dallas cheerleading for North Dallas High School and made a career out of cheerleading by establishing the National Cheerleaders Association in Dallas in

STADIUMS Stadiums have evolved dramatically from an open field surrounded by spectators and cars whose headlamps provided the first Friday night lights to durable venues like El Paso High School's Greco-Roman style Jones Stadium, one of the first concrete stadiums in the United States, built in 1916, to Allen High School's new $60 million facility. Other stadiums were constructed by the federal Works Progress Administration program in the 1930s and 1940s, including Fair Park Stadium in Childress and the Tomato Bowl in Jacksonville. Playing field surfaces have gone from dirt to natural grass to artificial turf while primitive scorekeeping mechanisms have advanced to electronic scoreboards with video screens.

MARCHING BANDS The marching band is an essential element of the pageantry, providing the music for the national anthem and each school's alma mater and fight song while offering musically spirited grandstand support during the game to en-

Allen HS band © 2007
Scott Yarberry, Yarberry Photography

monitoring the game clock and play clock. Also called refs, or zebras, officials keep the game civil. Although officials are paid for every game they call, it is a hobby for most officials, a surprising number of whom are employed in education or in law. They work specific regions in the state, clustered into districts.

More than 5,000 members of the Texas Association of Sports Officials (TASO) oversee Texas high school football games. TASO provides rule books to members, conducts workshops, and distributes written examinations to be administered annually.

CHEERLEADERS Cheerleaders are the motivators of school spirit. They lead the student body and fans in organized cheers, make signs and banners, organize pep rallies, and provide unconditional support to the team. Other than football players, they are the most visible personalities at high school football games. Cheerleading requires physical ability

1948 and organizing the nation's first cheerleading camp at Sam Houston State College in 1949 to improve skills and teach new routines. Herkimer created the first company for cheerleader uniforms and supplies and the Spirit Stick, which is awarded to exceptional cheerleaders at summer camps. He patented the pom-pom, the fuzzy paper balls that cheerleaders and dance teams use to emphasize hand motions. He is best known for the Herkie Jump, one of the most enduring physical moves in cheerleading, in which the cheerleader leaps, thrusts one leg forward and one leg back while making a punching motion with one hand; and for promoting cheerleading as an activity around the world.

The Crew, or the Gang, is a relatively new addition to the spirit corps on the sidelines. Composed of students sometimes wearing overalls or goofy clothes, they carry the flags after touchdowns or do pushups in the end zone, help blow up the inflatable tunnel, and assist cheerleaders and mascots in leading cheers.

ergize the team. The halftime show is performed by both schools' bands which play musical instruments while marching in synchronized movement, augmented by the color guard and drill/dance team.

There are two main styles of Texas high school marching bands – military and corps. Military style is more traditional, marching shoulder-to-shoulder in rigid precision in long strides – six steps for every five yards – which is still favored in East Texas. Corps style, which gained popularity in the 1950s and is now the predominant form in Texas high schools, is defined by a shorter stride – eight steps for every five yards – and a show in which the band makes geometric formations on the field. More recently, elaborate halftime shows have built upon the corps style to incorporate intricate designs, patterns, and curvilinear steps with flags, dancers, and props. The result is almost the scale of a Broadway production, with some marching bands hiring professional arrangers to produce their shows.

Competition between marching bands during halftime can be just as fierce as the football game.

In 1983, the UIL recognized that fact by creating stand alone marching band competitions. Every other year, marching bands participate in district, regional, area, and state competitions for each classification. Bands are judged on intonation, musicianship and marching competencies. Each band must assemble their equipment on the field in four minutes, perform for eight minutes, and break down their gear in two minutes. Bands compete throughout the fall at other local, regional, and national competitions including meets organized by the United States Scholastic Band Association and Bands of America, where L.D. Bell of Hurst was crowned 2007 Grand National Champion and Westfield High of Houston were the 2003 national winners.

DANCE/DRILL TEAMS Dance/Drill teams provide additional choreography for halftime shows and show support by forming victory lines on the field before games and doing orchestrated cheers in the

movement of Texas's population over the past century from rural to urban to suburban and from a segregated tri-ethnic society to a rich, spicy chili, mixing old and new Texan cultures.

In the first half of the 20th century, small towns and cities with vibrant economies, such as Waco, Abilene, Breckenridge, Lufkin, Tyler Longview, and Marshall dominated the sport. With the rise of cities following World War II, schools in Dallas, Houston, Austin, and San Antonio excelled. Since the 1980s, suburban schools with new facilities and growing population bases have risen to the top, including Judson and Smithson Valley outside San Antonio; Plano, Duncanville, Lucas-Lovejoy, Allen, Celina, and Richardson near Dallas; Euless Trinity, Southlake Carroll, and Aledo by Fort Worth; Katy, The Woodlands, Stratford, Sealy, and Willowridge near Houston; and Reagan, Pflugerville, Westlake, Cedar Park, and Lake Travis near Austin.

The UIL organizes its 1,300 plus member schools into conferences based on enrollment and into dis-

from higher classifications to Six Man as their student bodies have declined.

PRIVATE SCHOOLS The Texas Catholic Interscholastic League (TCIL) was founded in 1948 as the governing body for athletics at private Catholic schools in Texas, changing its name to the Texas Christian Interscholastic League to welcome non-Catholic private schools before folding in 1999. TCIL football was dominated by Dallas Jesuit High and Houston Strake Jesuit High. The Texas Association of Private and Parochial Schools (TAPPS), the governing body for athletic and academic contests for more than 220 member non-public high schools in Texas, was founded in 1978. TAPPS has five classifications for Eleven Man football and two for Six Man football. The Southwest Preparatory Conference (SPC) founded in 1952, oversees 16

James Madison HS Dollies, San Antonio Photo by Allison Crain, Courtesy St. Edward's University, Austin, ca. 2010

grandstands. Inspired by the drum and bugle corps that led armies into battle, traditional drill teams have evolved into dance teams that typically perform one of two styles. The classic high kicking cowgirl style was inspired by Gussie Nell Davis, founder of the Greenville High School Flaming Flashes in 1928 and later the Kilgore Junior College Rangerettes. The cowgirl outfits favored by many dance/drill teams in Texas high schools are heavily influenced by the Kilgore Rangerettes, even though the fashion had already been popularized by the San Antonio Jefferson High School Lassos in 1932, eight years before the Rangerettes came into existence. The modern jazz dance style can be traced back to Dr. Kay Teer Crawford, founder of the Edinburg High School Sargeanettes in 1930. Both styles emphasize precision, coordinated kicks, hand routines with and without pom poms, jump splits, and contagions, or ripples, while stressing femininity, poise, and discipline.

DYNASTIES: RURAL TO URBAN TO SUBURBAN
The evolution of high school football mirrors the

tricts and regions for each classification based on geography. Classifications are Six Man, 1A, 2A, 3A, 4A, and 5A. At the end of the regular season each conference is split into two divisions based on enrollment for playoffs.

To find the powerhouse schools in Texas, just follow the money. Historically, the most successful high school football programs have benefited from the local economy, be they oil patch boom towns in the 1920s-1950s, communities adjacent to military bases and industrial plants, wealthy enclaves, booming suburbs, resort towns, and schools that receive tax dollars from wind farms in West Central Texas and lignite coal plants in East Texas. Some of the strongest schools in the early days of Texas high school football were located in rural parts of East and West Texas.

Population also influences schools. Football at Katy High School and Pflugerville High School has grown with their communities, transitioning from Six Man to 5A over the course of a few decades. Conversely, some West Texas schools have dropped

member schools in Texas and two in Oklahoma. Thirty-two schools belong to the Texas Christian Athletic Fellowship (TCAF), founded in 1984. The Texas Christian Athletic League (TCAL), founded in 1991, has 72 member schools.

DISTRICTS AND CONFERENCES Every two years in February, the UIL realigns districts and conferences, reflecting changes in school enrollment. The realignment of districts and adjustment of classifications have a major impact on school budgets, especially in rural areas in the western part of the state where travel within some districts exceeds two hundred miles between schools. For example, when Amarillo plays San Angelo, the drive is over 300 miles one way. Realignment can influence traditional rivalries and can determine a school's fortunes depending on whether competing schools are strong or weak. The UIL's redistricting methodology utilizes state maps, push pins, and rubber bands to determine districts. The results inspire formal protests and even lawsuits.

PLAYOFFS UIL has overseen championships since 1920 when all schools competed in the same classification. Between 1922 and 1925 UIL created two classifications based on enrollment, with only class A teams competing for state and B schools limited to bi-district championships. In 1939, conferences 1A, 2A, and B were established. Conference 2A played to state, 1A played to the regional level, and B to the bi-district level. In 1948, conference 1A started playing to state as well, and a separate city conference was added. When the city conference was dropped in 1951, that left 1A, 2A, 3A, and now 4A, all of which played to the state level, while B played to regional. The classifications held steady until 1980 when the 5A conference was added. Over the course of the 1990s, classes 5A, 4A, 3A, and 2A split into Division I and Division II to equalize enrollment within the division of each conference. The 1A Eleven Man and 1A Six Man conferences followed suit in 2006. Today, each district sends its top four schools into playoffs, the two schools with the largest enrollment going into Division I playoffs, and the two schools with smaller enrollments going into Division II. The exception is 1A Eleven Man, 1A Six Man, and 2A which divide districts into Division I and Division II at the start of the season.

INNOVATORS Coaches have historically used creative thinking to come up with new strategies to facilitate their work. Sometimes their innovations have resonated far beyond the field where they coach, impacting college and professional football teams.

Felton "Pooch" Wright, coach of the Ballinger Bearcats during the 1930s, created many tools to better his team's performance. In order to encourage his quarterback to train during the summer, Wright constructed a spring-loaded snapping machine that would hike the ball to the quarterback whenever he wasn't doing chores on the family's isolated ranch. Wright also developed the Ballinger Blocking Board, a complement to the regular scoreboard that gave credit to the unheralded linemen on the team by showing spectators whether or not the blocker fulfilled his assignment on an offensive play. Members of the JV squad sat inside the scoreboard and tracked individual players, giving them a green light if they performed as instructed, or a red light if they failed. The invention wasn't particularly accurate due to the human factor. One of the board operators, JV player Johnny Earnshaw, admitted, "I never gave a red light [to the lineman he was watching]; he'd of beat the crap out of me if I did." Wright produced a brochure for the Ballinger Blocking Board in the hopes that he could produce them for other schools, and brought SMU head coach Matty Bell and other college and high school coaches to Ballinger for demonstrations.

Emory Bellard is best known for introducing the wishbone offense to college football. The wishbone offense lines up two running backs behind the quarterback, allowing the quarterback to hand off the ball, run with the ball, or pitch back the ball to a trailing running back. While Bellard's signature offensive formation was perfected during his time as a college coach, he formulated the offense while coaching the Breckenridge Buckaroos, leading them to two state championships in 1958 and 1959. Bellard also won a state title at San Angelo Central and two Class B regional championships at Ingleside. While still at Breckenridge, Bellard asked Spectrum Scoreboards to design a timer to better organize practice. The EB 1 and EB 2 timers were created and are still sold by Spectrum to high schools and colleges across the nation.

Austin High Coach Stan Lambert developed the two platoon system which used different players for offense and for defense. He employed the use of Walkie-talkies to communicate with other coaches. Lambert was the first coach to fly his team to a game, sending them from Austin to San Antonio for a playoff game in 1946. And he wrote the Quarterback's Blue Book, the first published guide that addressed how to improve skills specific to the position.

HEALTH AND SAFETY Football has evolved from the days when players were forbidden to drink water during practice to a sport with a critical interest in physiology, giving birth to Sports Medicine as an academic discipline. Today, strength and conditioning are part of every team's regimen while obesity, heart issues, nutrition, steroids and concussions have become part of the conversation. Most large high school football teams employ staff trainers augmented by student trainers. Smaller schools in remote parts of the state rely on traveling trainers as well as students. The trainers assess, manage, and rehabilitate player injuries. Before and after the game they tape ankles, wrists, and knees and apply ice and heat to sore muscles. During the game they hydrate and cool down players and tend to injuries. The Texas State Athletic Trainers' Association promotes and advances the athletic training profession, including secondary school athletic trainers. Texas became the first state to require athletic trainers to meet specific standards of education, professionalism, and ethics in 1971. Individuals are licensed by the State Advisory Board of Athletic Trainers, a division of the Texas Department of Health.

DIVERSITY Texas High School Football cuts across boundaries and divisions that normally divide people from one another. A person's race, religion, wealth, prominence in the community, and academic strength no longer matter once inside the stadium. It's how one participates that matters. The even playing field has provided a stage for African Americans and Mexican Americans in Texas, as well as other ethnic groups not traditionally associated with the game of football, including Vietnamese Americans such as Dat Nguyen of Rockport, Tongan players from Euless Trinity, and representatives of newly arrived immigrant communities from India, Africa, Asia, and South America.

ACROSS BORDERS For the past ten years, teams from two schools in Monterrey, Nuevo Leon have crossed the border to play Texas high schools. The Tigres (Tigers) of Universidad Autonomic de Nuevo Leon Prep School and the Monterrey Prepa Tec Borregos (Rams) both scheduled games against Texas high schools in the 2010 season. Gustavo Adame, the assistant coach at Prepa Tec said the Borregos had been the national high school champions of Mexico for the past five years. "Five years ago we started playing border schools – McAllen, Mission, rolling Port Isabel and Rockport-Fulton. We're playing five 4A and 5A big schools this year," Adame said. "Five years from now, we'll come back and we'll beat Allen and give The Woodlands a good run."

SIX MAN Six Man football represents the soul of small town Texas. The scaled down version of the game, tailored for schools unable to field Eleven Man squads, is on a growth spurt due to the decline in population of small towns and rural areas and its popularity among new private and parochial schools with small student bodies. In 2009, 127 UIL schools and 109 private schools including 56 TAPPS schools fielded Six Man teams, more than any other state.

Six Man is a faster game requiring more versatility and less specialization. Every player has to be ready to serve several purposes on a given play. Fans love Six Man for its high scoring offenses and low-tech values, and for the dearth of pomp and glitz, the polar opposite of big time 5A and 4A Texas high school football. In Six Man football, the concession stand is the guy who's fired up his portable barbecue pit and dumped some drinks in an ice chest. A fan yelling can be heard by the team, the coaches, the whole stadium. And when the home team scores, supporters who are watching the game in their cars and pickups honk their horns and flash their lights.

ACADEMICS For the first 90 years of Texas high school football, performance on the field often came at the expense of classroom studies. At many schools, outstanding players didn't have to worry about their grades as long as they played well. House Bill 72, signed into law on July 13, 1984, established academic standards in order to participate in extracurricular activities in Texas public schools. Nicknamed "No Pass, No Play," the law was championed by Dallas billionaire H. Ross Perot, head of the Select Committee on Public Education, who told the Legislative Council that "extracurricular activities should be put into perspective. They can no longer be the forces that disrupt our classes and dominate our schools." The law was unpopular among many football supporters, some of whom argued that coaches had their own policy of "No Pass, No Play." Jimmy Carmichael, quarterback of the 1970 3A state champion Brownwood Lions recalled that under coach Gordon Wood, "If we failed any course, we knew we were

Midland HS fans
Photo by Emma Wellen,
Courtesy Midland High School,
ca. 2010

off the team, no exceptions." Nonetheless, the bill has been an effective way of making academics the first priority for all who participate in UIL-sponsored competitions.

THE MEDIA The vast number of participants in Friday night football would be meaningless if not for the passion exhibited by their supporters and the media that cover the sport. With ample assistance from newspapers, television, radio, blogs, websites and books, Texas high school football, along with marching bands, dance/drill teams, mascots, and cheerleaders, is bigger and more popular than ever, increasingly recognized nationally and internationally as part of the Texas identity.

Texas newspapers have been telling the story of Texas high school football since its inception, first reported by the *Galveston Daily News* in 1892. Newspapers responded to the sport's growing popularity by expanding coverage and recruiting correspondents among its readership to report scores. In 1929, Harold Ratliff of the *Cleburne Press-Review* selected the first All-State high school football team. Studying the Saturday morning score boxes continues to be a ritual for readers of sports sections of every major newspaper in Texas, with expanded reporting online.

In 1936, eleven radio stations formed the Magnolia network, sponsored by Magnolia Petroleum, to broadcast the state quarterfinal games. The network grew into the nation's largest for high school football. WBAP-TV, Channel 5, broadcast the first televised high school football game in Texas from Fort Worth's Farrington Field in September 1948, pitting the hometown Paschal Panthers against the Amarillo Golden Sandies.

Today, Texas high school football games are broadcast on television and radio stations, as well as on websites across the state. Fox Sports Southwest broadcast the 2010 UIL state championships on television and online. Internet websites have made it possible to extend coverage of regions, classifications, and specific schools, and have provided additional content for newspapers and radio and television.

Dave Campbell, sports editor of the *Waco Tribune-Herald*, debuted *Texas Football* magazine in 1960, devoting the entire annual issue to previewing every Texas high school and college football team. Each year's new edition is released at the Texas Sports Museum in Waco with the now-retired Campbell on hand to sign autographs, in one of the most anticipated annual events in Texas sports. Regarded the "Bible of Texas high school football," *Texas Football* is complemented by a website and by the Texas Football Classic season opener games staged in San Antonio's Alamodome.

The local high school football team is one of the most popular subjects in Texas literature, signifying the pastime as defining community. Schools as disparate as Plano, Katy, Abilene, and Port Neches-Groves and coaches including Cotton Miles and Gordon

Dallas Colored High School football team Courtesy *Dallas Historical Society, Used by permission, ca. 1909*

Wood have had their stories published in book form. Beginning in the 1960s, Harold Ratliff, the state sports editor for the Associated Press, and Bill McMurray of the Houston Chronicle wrote the first extensive histories of Texas high school football, giving birth to a literary genre. Ratliff's *Autumn's Mightiest Legions: History of Texas Schoolboy Football* and *Texas Schoolboy Football: Champions in Action*, along with McMurray's *Texas High School Football* remain classics.

FRIDAY NIGHT LIGHTS In 1988, a Philadelphia sportswriter named H. G. Bissinger spent a season following the Odessa Permian Panthers football team. He got to know the coaches, the players, the players' families, the boosters, and the West Texas oil city of Odessa. Three years later, *Friday Night Lights: A Town, A Team, and A Dream* was published. The book put Permian High and Odessa on the map, stirring up controversy over Bissinger's unflinchingly honest depiction of high school football in West Texas and how a community lives through its team. The book, which detailed racial tensions and the pressures placed on players, painted a darker picture of Texas high school football. Bissinger was persona non grata in Odessa and even received death threats. Nonetheless, his book made Texas high school football a national obsession, spawning a movie and a television series.

In 2004, a film version of the book directed by Peter Berg and starring Billy Bob Thornton as the Coach was released. It tried, but did not quite succeed to capture the contradictions of football as the only thing that mattered in an isolated, economically struggling community in West Texas. Two years later, Berg adapted the story to television and the TV version of "Friday Night Lights" debuted. Set in the fictional Texas town of Dillon, its realistic storylines managed to evoke the essence of football and community in the American heartland. The critically acclaimed series ran for five seasons on NBC and DIRECTV until 2011.

FANS Fans make the game. Whether it is football hounds with seats on the 50 yard line, middle school kids flirting under the grandstands, or toddlers dressed in jerseys and cheerleader uniforms, the football game is the social event of the week. But, nothing compares to being a parent or relative of a player, band member, dancer, cheerleader, or mascot and watching your child participate. A parent, aunt, uncle, cousin, or family friend can provide support by consoling a son after a disappointing game, praising a daughter for her outstanding performance, photographing and filming their every move, wearing a button that identifies their child, or simply offering "good game" at the end of the evening. Many parents are also heavily involved with booster clubs. Booster clubs are non-profit organizations that provide financial and physical support to football teams, marching bands, dance/drill teams, cheerleaders, and other elements of Friday night football. They raise money with concession sales, raffles, auctions, bake sales, and by selling t-shirts and other items associated with the

school and football team. Boosters staff the concession stands, help with the inflatable tunnels, assist in parking, ticket-taking, seating, and whatever else is necessary.

Ultimate fans, called Football Hounds, are that rare breed who follow Texas high school football by traveling around the state in search of a good game, including a rabid subset known as Six Man Hounds. The Hound of Hounds is Bennie Cotton. A resident of the southeast Texas town of Orangefield, Cotton racks up thousands of miles on the odometer of his pickup truck in pursuit of what he calls "the best football in the world."

Cotton got the bug when he saw his first Orangefield Bobcats football game in 1941 at the age of nine; he later played for the Bobcats' Six Man team. He started driving around the state in 1960. Since then, Cotton has lived and breathed high school football from the first week of the season, to the state championships in December, attending as many as 65 games in a single season, and more than 2,000 games since his trek began.

Cotton is easily recognized by his gray beard, his hand-painted gimme cap listing the winningest high schools in Texas with their school colors, and the well-thumbed log he carries with him to detail his adventures. He has never calculated the mileage he accrues every season, out of fear it might discourage him from continuing to pursue his passion.

LIFE'S LESSONS For all of the passion that goes into Friday night football, there are plenty of people who are quick to point out the downsides to the zeal with which Texans embrace the sport. Jealous cheerleader moms, heart attacks, concussions, spinal injuries, and even death on the field and in the stands are part of the landscape. Then, there are the excessive amounts of money spent on facilities, the priority given to sports over academics in school funding, coaches who are paid more than principals, and the disparity between rich schools and poor schools. These are controversial issues in Texas high school football, as are cheating, gambling, steroids, and prayer in schools. But, the controversy stirred up by the culture of high school football helps to fuel the culture itself. The drama that such controversy provides is one reason why Texas high school football is a state obsession and a national interest.

Texas High School Football is more than winning and losing. Life's lessons are taught and learned on Friday nights. Every participant in the spectacle can appreciate the value of teamwork, sacrifice, and dedication. After the game, everyone goes their separate ways, but those qualities remain. Some individuals carry the lessons learned from the high school football experience with them throughout their lives. The participants on the field and in the stands know that football just doesn't mirror life. For them, football is life. All the rest is just details.

JOE NICK PATOSKI
Guest Curator

THE HALLWAY OF HISTORY

92

1892 On December 24, Ball High football team plays Galveston Rugbys. The game "excited a degree of attention sufficient to draw to the scene of contest a large concourse of people," according to the *Galveston Daily News*. Rugbys win 14-0.

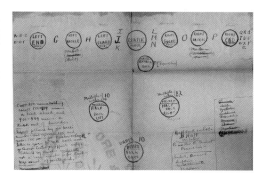

1900 October 12 game between St. Matthew's Grammar School of Dallas and the Wall School of Honey Grove in Fannin County is 1st played between 2 Texas high schools. Wall wins, 5-0.

1913 In December, Sam Houston Lions defeat Comanche 20-0 at Clark Field in Austin in 1st Texas high school championship football game. The game was not sanctioned by UIL officials.

1918 Jacksonville, Dallas and Bryan Street, Oak Cliff and other schools cancel season due to outbreak of Spanish flu brought home by soldiers returning from World War I.

1922 John Drew "Boody" Johnson, is aka "The Waco Wildcat," runs, punts, and dropkicks Waco High to 13-10 win over Abilene Eagles. Johnson called the greatest high school football player in Texas history in 1968 by Harold Ratliff, the sportswriter known as Mr. Schoolboy Football.

1925 C.O. Wilson organizes first Nederland football team and obtains cyclone fencing, lighting, and bleachers for stadium at 220 So. 12th.

1926 John Phillip Sousa, "The March King," comes to Abilene to lead the Eagle Marching Band of Abilene High School, formed by new director Raymond T. "Prof" Bynum. Prof Bynum would become known as Father of Texas High School Marching Bands, credited with pioneering marching band pageantry during halftime at football games. Through his efforts, Abilene High is 1st in Texas to make music part of academic curriculum.

1927 Amarillo High organizes its 1st marching band with W.A. Criswell as its student director.

Waco Tigers win their 4th state title in their 6th championship game appearance, establishing Tigers as the dominant team of 1920s.

1929 Elizabeth (Smitty) Smith forms Red Hussars, 1st all-female drum and bugle corps in Texas, at Port Arthur High School. The Red Hussars, led by drum majorette Hazel Dunham, are formed to replace the pep squad. Band director O. L. Pop Lantz writes original composition for Hussars, "Here We Come," and the girls gain statewide notoriety.

1930 Texas High School Coaches Association is founded.

1936 Sylvester High beats Dowell High, 14-0, at Rotan on September 29 in 1st 6-man football game played in Texas. 4 schools in Fisher County form 1st 6-man football league in state.

1936 Amarillo Sandies beat Kerrville Tivy 19-6 to take state for 3rd consecutive state championship under Coach Blair Cherry, who later coached at the University of Texas and inspired Tom Landry to wear a fedora while coaching.

1938 UIL formalizes AA, A, and B conferences based on enrollment. After organizing spring game between Martindale and Prairie Lea, UIL creates 6-man football classification; more than 100 schools are playing by 1939.

1939 Lubbock Westerners' finish miracle season by beating Waco Tigers and dean of Texas coaches, Paul Tyson, 20-14, at Cotton Bowl to win state after Coach Weldon Bailey Chapman passes away in November.

1940 I.M. Terrell High School of Fort Worth defeats Austin Anderson High School, 26-0, at Farrington Field in Fort Worth to win 1st state championship in new league for African-American high schools called Texas Interscholastic League of Colored Schools. Farrington Field mandates west side of stadium is reserved for white fans.

1940 E.C. Lerma becomes 1st Mexican-American football coach for a Texas high school at Benavides.

1941 Mission Eagles, coached by Bob Martin and led by quarterback Tom Landry, go undefeated, outscoring opponents 268-7 and winning South Texas 1A regional championship by beating Hondo Owls, 33-0. Martin, who played high school football for storied Breckenridge Buckaroos, instills toughness and demands discipline from his players, especially Landry who lives next door to Martin, by banning soft drinks, imposing a curfew, and discouraging team members from dating.

53

1953 Sugar Land Gators' single wing quarterback Ken Hall, aka The Sugarland Express, sets 17 national schoolboy records including rushing (11,232 yards), points per game (32.9), career scoring (899), single season rushing (4,045), single season points (395) and total offense (14,558 yards), leading Gators to regional championship, beating Magnolia, 13-6. Hall, regarded as greatest high school football player ever, still holds national records for season rushing yards, average yards per game, and points per game.

1954-56 Abilene High War Eagles, coached by Chuck Moser, win 3 consecutive 4A state championships, winning 49 consecutive games and outscoring opponents 1,791-283 despite competing in District 4A-3, Little Southwest Conference, getting Team of the Century recognition from *Dallas Morning News*.

Little SWC, named in 1951 by a sportswriter because it resembles in intensity the university-level Southwest Conference composed almost exclusively of Texas colleges, is comprised of high schools from largest cities in West Texas - Midland, Odessa, Abilene, San Angelo Central, Lubbock, Amarillo, Pampa and Borger - and is arguably toughest high school football league in U.S. Little SWC draws crowds upwards of 20,000 for district games. By 2011, member schools will have competed in state championship game 32 times.

1957 Pflugerville, Prairie Lea, Hutto, Kyle, and Buda begin playing 8-man football as a transition between 6-man and 11-man.

1957 Highland Park Scots win state 4A championship, after tying Abilene and advancing on penetrations in the semi-final game.

1900-1920 The sport explodes in popularity over next 2 decades. High schools from Orange to El Paso form football teams.

1920s Pep squads form at more than 150 Texas high schools to support football teams with organized cheers and coordinated hand motions, sometimes marching in military-style precision on the field during halftime. Some pep squads in East Texas feature wooden rifle-shaped batons that are twirled in unison by leaders marching in a ceremonial strut.

1921 On January 8, Cleburne and Houston Heights tied 0-0 at Clark Field in Austin in 1st sanctioned state championship. The game decided state title between champions of North and South Texas.

21

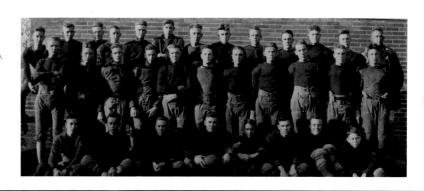

1932 Jefferson High School in San Antonio unveils the Lassos, an all-female dance/drill team who strut onto the football field in gray Stetson western hats, red satin blouses, blue flannel skirts, brown belts and oxford shoes, with Lasso officers wearing boots. They twirl ropes in unison, forming the initial "TJ." They appear on the cover of *Life* magazine and are twice featured in movies filmed on campus by Twentieth Century Fox. They travel by train to 1939 World's Fair in New York and enjoy tea at White House with First Lady Eleanor Roosevelt.

1932 With 12 players on the roster, the undersized, undermanned Masonic Home Mighty Mites from Fort Worth's Masonic Home orphanage, coached by Rusty Russell and his inventive spread offense, tie Corsicana, 0-0, losing state championship on penetrations, but winning hearts with the orphans' determined play.

1934 Chester Nebraska High School coach Stephen Epler invents 6-man football. Wheaties supports "new sport."

34

1934 London High School opens first stadium with electric lights, giving birth to Friday night lights.

Landry responds by rushing for 21 touchdowns and passing for 6 more touchdowns over course of season, including 2 touchdown passes and a 64-yard run for a touchdown against Hondo. Landry makes All-Valley team and is invited to participate in Texas High School Football All-Star game before earning an athletic scholarship to attend University of Texas.

43

1943 World War II leaves football rosters depleted and ushers in new era for girls in bands and cheerleading.

1943 Texas School for the Deaf Rangers wins 3rd consecutive National Deaf Prep championship title.

1945 A record crowd of 45,790 jam Cotton Bowl to watch Highland Park and Waco play to a 7-7 tie in state championship game.

1948 Frankie Groves of Stinnett Rattlers becomes 1st girl to play Texas high school football.

1951 UIL drops city conference and adds 4A and 3A classifications to existing 2A and 1A conferences playing for state championships while Class B and 6–man conferences vie for regional championships.

1958 Breckenridge Buckaroos win 4th state 3A title in 8 years running a precursor to Coach Emory Bellard's wishbone offense, beating Kingsville 48-14. With an enrollment of 400 students and a roster of as few as 30 players, Bellard, and coaches Cooper Robbins and Joe Kerbel before him, establish dynasty with players such as linebacker Jerry Tubbs and running back Jakie Sandefer. *Fort Worth Star Telegram* votes 1958 Buckaroos as Texas's Team of the Century.

1959 Katy Tigers win 1st state championship as 1A school, beating Sundown Roughnecks, 16-6.

1960 Ray Miller Buccaneers, coached by Pete Ragus and powered by running back Johnny Roland, become 1st fully integrated state champs. Coach Ragus is honored as Texas High School Football Coach of the Year.

1960 Coles wins PVIL 3A and Corpus Christi Catholic High wins the TCIL small school division. Miller follows crosstown rival Ray High, which won 1959 4A state crown. The Battlin' Buccaneers endure racial epithets and insults from other schools' fans in out-of-town games on their way to finals. The championship game against Wichita Falls High Coyotes is 1st Texas high school football game to be televised statewide. Johnny Roland follows Miller grad Bobby Smith as 1st two African-Americans to make All-State.

1961 Donna Redskins triumph, 28-21 over Iowa Park Hawks in Austin for 2A crown, the 1st and only Rio Grande Valley team to ever win state.

1963 Gerald Beal, Jr. coaches Kirkpatrick to victory over Fidelity for 2nd consecutive 3A PVIL crown, the last state championship team for a Fort Worth school.

1964 Chuck Curtis becomes 1st coach to win 3 consecutive state titles at 2 schools with Garland Owls' 2nd straight 4A title after leading Jacksboro Tigers to state 2A crown in 1962.

64

1964 UIL opens membership to all schools, including PVIL schools, marking beginning of end of segregated high school football in Texas. Integration did not happen immediately. Carver stayed open until 1970 after winning District 2-AAA championship in 1967.

1968 Lubbock Estacado Matadors, the city's 1st integrated high school, beats Refugio for state 4A championship to become only Texas high school to win state the 1st year the school opened.

1969 Wichita Falls wins their 6th state title taking 4A crown led by Ronnie Littleton, the 1st African-American star for storied Coyotes

---

1977 Record crowd of 49,953 bears witness to Plano Wildcats edging Port Neches-Groves Indians, 13-10, at Texas Stadium in Irving in 4A state finals.

1983 Daingerfield Tigers, coached by Dennis Alexander, finish one of the greatest seasons of any team anywhere, taking state 3A championship by beating Sweeny, 42-0, to go undefeated in 16 games, outscoring the opposition 631-8 (none allowed by defense) and allowing 0 points in playoffs.

1983-84 1st UIL state marching band competitions are held, forever altering the halftime show. Winners are Asherton, Dripping Springs, Denver City, Georgetown, and Laredo Nixon, with DeSoto winning Governor's Cup.

1985 Houston Yates Lions roll over Odessa Permian Panthers, 38-0, for 5A championship, becoming 1st post-integration African-American majority high school to win state.

85

1985 Coach Gordon Wood retires with 396 victories and 9 state titles after head coaching stints at Rule, Roscoe, Seminole, Winters, Stamford, Victoria, and Brownwood where he spent 26 years, winning 7 state championships. He led the Stamford Bulldogs to consecutive state titles in 1955 and 1956 as well.

1987 Robert Strait breaks almost every rushing record except Ken Hall's, as Cuero Gobblers run over Halletsville Brahmas, 37-13, for state 3A title.

90

1990 UIL introduces Division I and II to 5A playoffs, eventually splitting every classification into 2 divisions based on enrollment to allow more teams into playoffs and create parity between schools with similar enrollments.

Initially, 3 teams advance to playoffs, with a 4th school added later. The 2 larger schools compete in Division I playoffs, the 2 smaller schools compete in Division II. The exception is 3A schools, which continue to send 3 teams in each district into playoffs, the school with highest enrollment going into Division I, the 2 schools with smaller enrollments going into Division II.

1990 Rodney Thomas leads Groveton Indians to their 2nd consecutive 2A title and 3rd state championship in 7 years, beating DeLeon 25-19, while rushing for 3,701 yards in his last season, 2nd only to Ken Hall, and becoming 1st Texas schoolboy running back to rush for at least 100 yards in all 16 games.

1991 Fort Hancock Mustangs, coached by Danny Medina, win their 4th straight 6-man state title and their 5th in 6 years, decimating Christoval, 64-14, in title game at Wink.

FALCONS

1993 UIL lifts ban on girls practicing and participating in varsity football, allowing Amanda Heathcott to play football for Veribest Falcons in 1997.

94

1994 Southlake Carroll Dragons win their 72nd consecutive regular season game, a Texas high school record.

1994 Plano wins 7th state championship, beating Katy, 28-7, for 5A Division I title.

1997 Sealy Tigers win their 4th consecutive state 3A title under Coach T. J. Mills, beating Commerce, 28-21, and staking claim to Titletown, Texas as first 11-man team in Texas high school history to win 4 championships in a row.

02

2002 Coach G. A. Moore became Texas high school football's winningest coach with 397 wins on November 8 when the Pilot Point Bearcats defeated Van Alstyne, 27-13. Moore reached this record at his alma mater, Pilot Point,

after coaching for 14 years at Celina where his Bobcats won 4 consecutive 2A Division II championships. He became the coach at Aubrey in 2009, and at the end of the 2010 season had recorded 422 victories.

2002-06 Former Port Arthur Thomas Jefferson High quarterback Todd Dodge coaches Southlake Carroll Dragons to 79-1 record and 4 5A Division II championships,

winning state titles in 2002, their 1st year competing in 5A, and in 2004, 2005, and 2006, with their "Air-Raid" offense. Carroll's only loss in 5 years is to Katy Tigers in 2003 5A Division II championship, 15-14. The 34-20 win over Katy for 2005 crown pits Dragon quarterback Greg McElroy against Katy's Andy Dalton, who respectively become starting quarterbacks at national champion Alabama and undefeated T.C.U.

Katy Sports
It's how you FINISH

1971 Marty Akins quarterback of Gregory-Portland Wildcats and son of Coach Ray Akins, kicks and misses a last-second 35-yard field goal attempt and G-P falls to Plano Wildcats, 21-20, for 3A title, which *Austin American-Statesman* sportswriter George Breazeale calls the best game he'd ever seen.

1972 UIL adds state championships for Class B, 6-man, and 8-man. 8-man football will be eliminated in 1975.

1973 The John Tyler Lions from Tyler roar to state 4A title behind prowess of Ronnie Lee and brute force of running back Earl Campbell, "a man among boys," besting Austin Reagan Raiders 21-14.

1974 Uwe von Schamann of Fort Worth Eastern Hills breaks barefooted kicker Tony Franklin of Fort Worth Arlington Heights' city schoolboy record of 51 yards, set earlier that season, with a 53-yard field goal in 1st quarter of playoff game against Heights, only to have Franklin break von Schamann's records in 4th quarter with a 58-yard boot for Yellow Jackets, sealing 24-6 win over Highlanders.

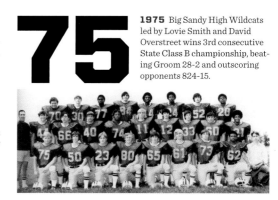

1975 Big Sandy High Wildcats led by Lovie Smith and David Overstreet wins 3rd consecutive State Class B championship, beating Groom 28-2 and outscoring opponents 824-15.

1987 Tim Brown of Notre Dame wins Heisman Trophy, earning Dallas Woodrow Wilson High School the reputation as "The High School Home of the Heisman," the only public high school to produce 2 winners of the prestigious annual award for most outstanding collegiate football player in U.S. Brown, Woodrow Class of 1984, joined Davey O'Brien, Woodrow Class of 1935, who won the Heisman in 1938 when he played for T.C.U.

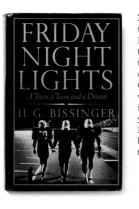

1989 Odessa Permian Panthers win 5A state beating Houston Aldine, 28-14, giving team a 122-11-6 record over the decade under leadership of Coach John Wilkins and Coach Gary Gaines. The 1989 win came after a disappointing loss at state in 1988, the year chronicled by Buzz Bissinger in the book that brought Friday night football to national attention.

1989 Coach Gordon Wood is recognized by several organizations as the Texas High School Football Coach of the Century and Brownwood Lions football stadium is named in his honor. For most of his career during which his teams won 80% of their games, Wood was assisted by Morris Southall and by former Stamford player Kenneth West. He was admired by Bear Bryant, Darrell Royal, Grant Teaff, and Bill Parcells, and was a friend of President Lyndon B. Johnson.

1998-00 Midland Lee Rebels, coached by John Parchman, achieve a 3-peat by defeating Austin Westlake, 33-21, winning 1 5A Division II championship and 2 5A Division I championships behind the legs of Cedric Benson who scores 15 touchdowns in the 3 title games.

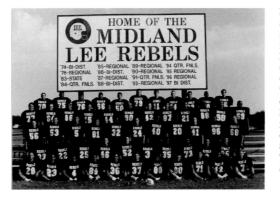

1998 First 7 on 7 football state tournament, after being approved by UIL in 1995, is an invitation-only affair in College Station where Southlake Carroll defeats 4A district rival Grapevine, 47-33. Texas State 7-on-7 Association Board is comprised of selected Texas high school coaches, but is a private organization not associated with UIL or Texas High School Coaches Association. The summer sport is played on a 45-yard field in t-shirts and shorts, does not allow blocking or tackling (a runner with the ball is down when they are touched by an opponent), forbids high school coaches from coaching the team or standing on the sidelines, and requires passing on all plays, giving rise to a new breed of quarterback in Texas high schools.

2008 Katy Tigers, under guidance of coaches Mike Johnston and Gary Joseph, win their 5th state title. They roll to 165-23 record in 13 seasons, winning 1 5A Division I and 4 5A Division II titles, establishing the school as the dominant 5A football program of the decade, despite 5 new high schools built within its district. The school began competing in 6-man conference in 1939 and gradually moved up to 2A, 3A, 4A, and 5A. Since 1986, Katy has only missed making playoffs twice.

2010 Jacksonville Fightin' Indians hold off Nacogdoches Dragons, 84-81, in 12th overtime to end longest game in high school history 5 ½ hours after it started.

2010 The Henderson Lions and Carthage Bulldogs, 2 schools that are 27 miles apart in District 3A-16, won the 3A Division I and Division II state championships respectively. (Carthage beat Henderson, 43-33, in district play).

2010 Lake Travis Cavaliers defeat Denton Ryan Raiders, 27-7, at Cowboys Stadium to become 3rd team in state history to win 4 consecutive high school football state championships, and 1st to win 4 straight in 4A or 5A. The Cavs take 4A Division I title in 2007 and Division II in 2008, 2009, in addition to 2010, guided by head coaches Jeff Dicus, Chad Morris, and Hank Carter, to become the dominant central Texas team of the modern era.

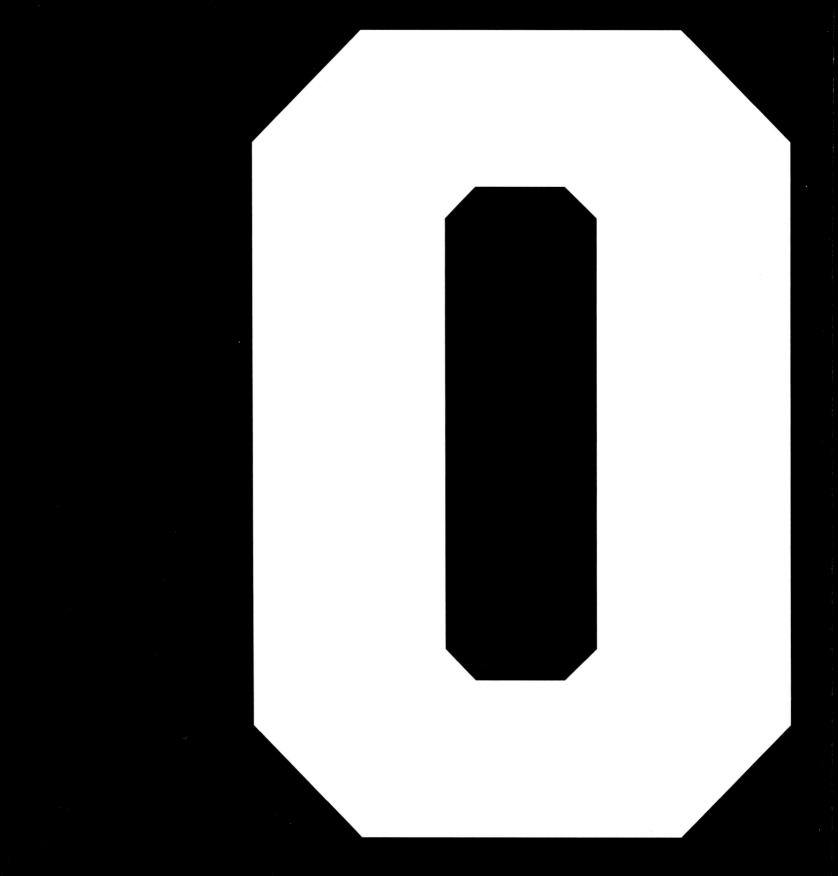

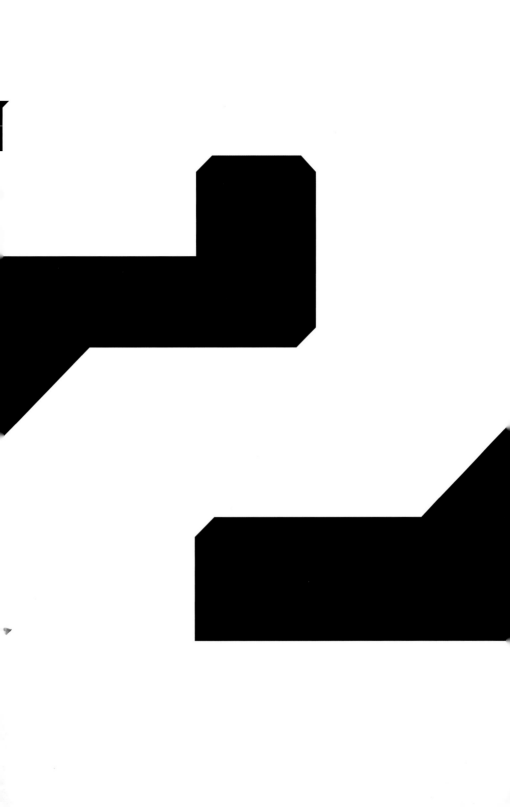

**01 DREW BREES
WESTLAKE HS JERSEY**
*Courtesy Texas High School
Football Hall of Fame, Waco,
ca. 1996*

02 SAN ANTONIO CHURCHILL HS HELMET WORN BY CODY CARLSON *Courtesy Texas High School Football Hall of Fame, Waco, ca. 1980-81*

03 FORT WORTH ARLINGTON HEIGHTS HS WRISTBAND PLAYBOOKS *Courtesy Chuck Taylor, Austin, ca. 1968*

04 WRISTBAND PLAYBOOK *Courtesy Westlake High School, Austin, ca. 2010*

05 MARTY AKINS' GREGORY-PORTLAND HS KICKING SHOE *Courtesy Texas High School Football Hall of Fame, Waco, ca. 1971*

06 JACK MILDREN'S COOPER HS UNIFORM PANTS *Courtesy Texas High School Football Hall of Fame, Waco, ca. 1967*

02

05

06

03

04

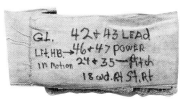

	Left Hash	White Deuce		Right Hash
		Runs	19	Lt Lasso 30
1	Rt Rope 31		20	Lt Loop 22
2	Rt Ring 23		21	Lt Rope 33 Book
3	Rt Lsso 32 Book		22	Lt Rope Tag 35 Book
4	Rt Lsso Tag 34 Book		23	Lt Loop 37
5	Rt Ring 36		24	Lt Ring 27 Opie Cross
6	Rt Lp 26 Opie Cross		25	Lt Rope 37 Opie
7	Rt Lsso 36 Opie		26	Lt Loop 39 Poedlb
8	Rt Ring 38 Poodle		27	
9			28	
10		Passes	29	Lt Ring 60
11	Rt Loop Odd 60		30	Lt Loop Odd 235 Fish
12	Rt Ring 234 Fish		31	Lt Lsso 72
13	Rt Rope 82		32	Lt Ring Flip 73
14	Rt Loop Flip 83		33	Lt Ring 234 Oklahoma
15	Rt Loop Odd 235 Oklahoma		34	Lt Loop 92
16	Rt Loop Odd 92	White One	35	Lt Ring 60
17	Rt Loop Odd 60		36	Lt Loop 62
18	Rt Ring Odd 62			

07 BROWNWOOD HS SIDELINE JACKET
Courtesy Gordon Wood Hall of Champions Museum, Brownwood, ca. 1940s

08 #2 DOWELL HS RED AND BLUE PATRIOTIC JERSEY
Courtesy Fischer County Pioneer Museum, Roby, ca. 1940s

09 CHUCK CURTIS'S COACHING SHIRT FROM JACKSBORO
Courtesy Texas High School Football Hall of Fame, Waco, ca. 1959-62

07

08

09

10 "W" WACO HS LETTER SWEATER

Courtesy Texas High School Football Hall of Fame, Waco, ca. 1920s

11 WACO HS LEATHER HELMET WORN BY TOMMY GLOVER

Courtesy Texas High School Football Hall of Fame, Waco, ca. 1927

12 NEW LONDON HS LEATHER HELMET

Courtesy New London Museum, ca. 1940s-1950s

13 WESTLAKE HS QUARTERBACK HELMET

Courtesy Westlake High School, Austin, ca. 1990s

10

11
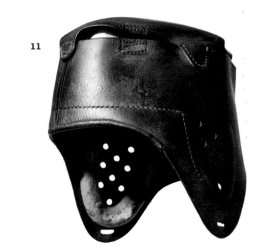

12

13

**14 EL PASO HS
LEATHER HELMET**

*Courtesy El Paso High School,
ca. 1910s*

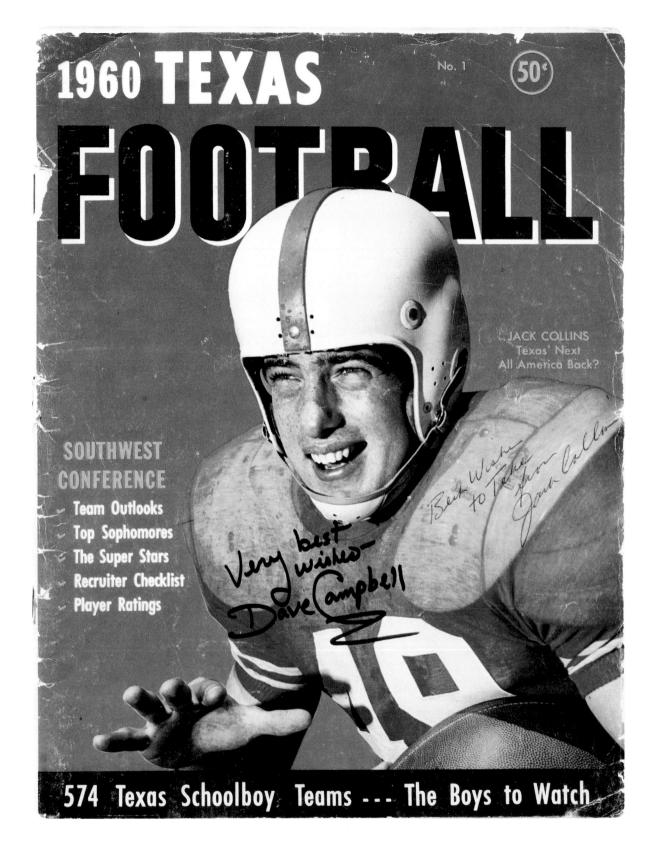

1960 TEXAS

No. 1

50¢

FOOTBALL

JACK COLLINS
Texas' Next
All America Back?

Best Wishes
To Teke
from Collins

SOUTHWEST
CONFERENCE

- Team Outlooks
- Top Sophomores
- The Super Stars
- Recruiter Checklist
- Player Ratings

Very best
wishes—
Dave Campbell

574 Texas Schoolboy Teams --- The Boys to Watch

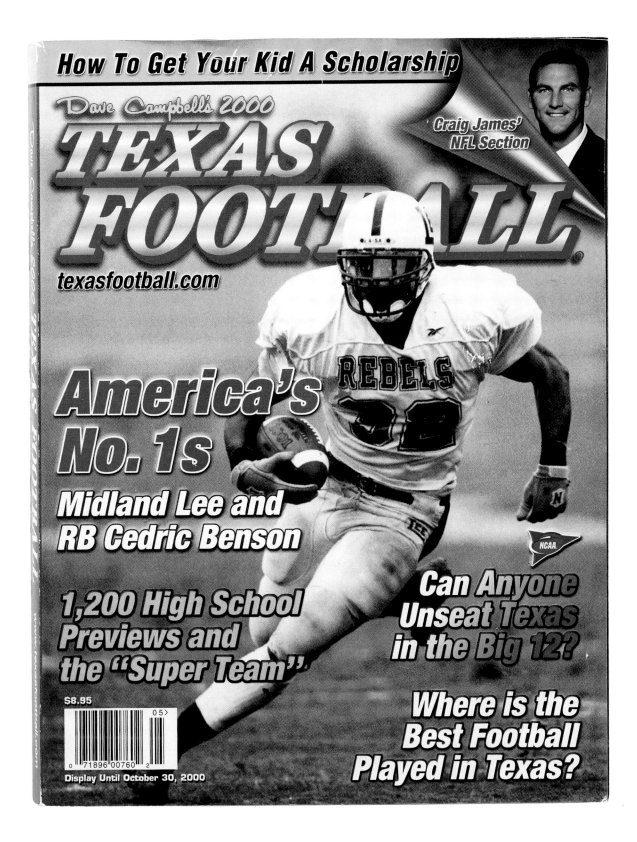

How To Get Your Kid A Scholarship

Dave Campbell's 2000
TEXAS FOOTBALL

texasfootball.com

Craig James'
NFL Section

America's No. 1s

Midland Lee and RB Cedric Benson

1,200 High School Previews and the "Super Team"

$8.95

Display Until October 30, 2000

0 71896 00760 2

05>

Can Anyone Unseat Texas in the Big 12?

Where is the Best Football Played in Texas?

17 DAVE CAMPBELL'S TEXAS FOOTBALL COVER WITH CEDRIC BENSON *Courtesy Teke Baker and Family, Round Rock, ca. 2000*

18 WILLIE MACK GARZA'S REFUGIO HS FOOTBALL JERSEY, #19 *Courtesy Refugio High School, ca. 1987*

19 JACK PARDEE'S CHRISTOVAL LETTER JACKET *Courtesy Texas High School Football Hall of Fame, Waco, ca. 1953*

20 THE QUARTERBACK'S BLUE BOOK *Courtesy Nancy Lewis and Kay Lambert, Austin, ca. 1946*

21 THE BALLINGER BLOCKING BOARD BOOKLET *Courtesy Texas High School Football Hall of Fame, Waco, ca. 1936*

22 TRAINER'S MEDICAL KIT FROM BRYAN HS *Courtesy Josh and Jamie Woodall, Bryan, ca. 1980s*

18

19

20

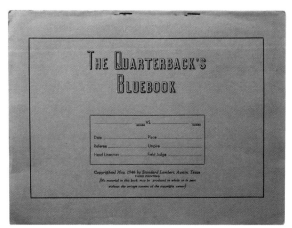

21

22

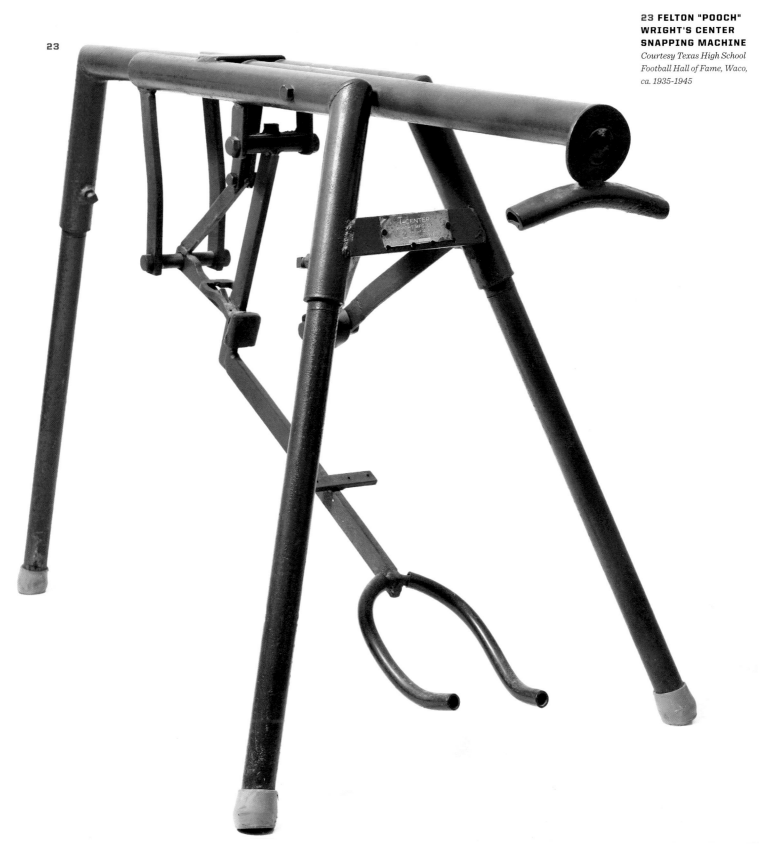

23 FELTON "POOCH" WRIGHT'S CENTER SNAPPING MACHINE
Courtesy Texas High School Football Hall of Fame, Waco, ca. 1935-1945

24 COACH FRANKIE BRAZOS'S WHISTLE
Courtesy Prairie View Interscholastic League Coaches Association, Austin, ca. 1950s

25 HOW TO PLAY SIX-MAN FOOTBALL BY STEPHEN EPLER
Courtesy Leman Saunders, Blackwell, ca. 1938

26 SIX-MAN FOOTBALL OFFICIAL RULE BOOK AND HOW TO PLAY HANDBOOK
Courtesy Leman Saunders, Blackwell, ca. 1941

27 TEXAS HIGH SCHOOL COACHES ASSOCIATION PROGRAM *Courtesy El Paso High School Alumni Association, ca. 1958*

24

Legendary Coach Frankie Brazos' Whistle
Donated by Walter Yates Sr.

25

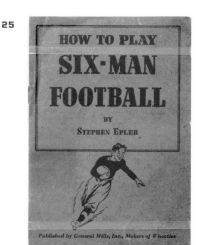

26

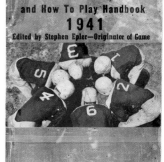

27

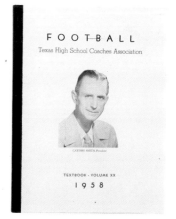

28 BENNIE COTTON'S LEDGER BOOK *Courtesy Bennie Cotton, Orangefield, ca. 1960 – 1981*

29 FELTON "POOCH" WRIGHT WITH PLAYER *Courtesy Texas High School Football Hall of Fame, Waco, ca. 1935-1945*

30 COACH LAMBERT AND AUSTIN HS TEAM BOARDING PLANE FOR PLAYOFF GAME *Courtesy The Brian W. Schenk Archives at Austin High School, ca. 1946*

31 GAME FILM REELS *Courtesy Abilene High School, ca. 1959-1989*

32 CUERO FIGHTIN' GOBBLERS 1987 STATE CHAMPIONS WIND-BREAKER *Courtesy Texas High School Football Hall of Fame, Waco, ca. 1987*

28

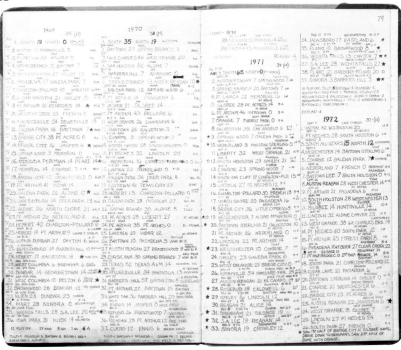

30

31

29

32

33 OFFICIAL'S UNIFORM
Courtesy Jim Peek, Commerce,
ca. early 1940s

34 OFFICIAL'S UNIFORM
Courtesy Roy Kimberlin, Plano,
ca. 2000s

35 DON MEREDITH'S MOUNT VERNON HS FOOTBALL JERSEY, #88 *Courtesy Franklin County Historical Association, Don Meredith Exhibit, Mount Vernon, ca. 1955*

36 EB 1 TIMER *Courtesy Texas High School Football Hall of Fame, Waco, ca. 1955*

37 FRANK WALKER'S HOUSTON WHEATLEY HS LETTER SWEATER *Courtesy Prairie View Interscholastic League Coaches Association, Austin, ca. 1930s*

38 DONNA REDSKINS STATE CHAMPION LETTER JACKET AND MEDALS *Courtesy Richard Avila and Luz Padriza, Donna, ca. 1961*

35

37

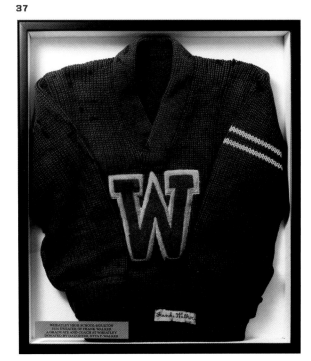

36

38

39 OFFICIAL'S HORN
Courtesy Conrad Turner and George Maxwell, Houston, ca. 1917

40 OFFICIAL'S RED AND WHITE PENALTY FLAG *Courtesy Ronnie Bennett, Beaumont, ca. 1960s*

39

40

41 OFFICIAL'S YELLOW PENALTY FLAG *Courtesy Roy Kimberlin, Plano, ca. 2000s*

42

43 EL PASO FOOTBALL TEAM PHOTOGRAPH
Courtesy El Paso High School, ca. 1908

44 AMANDA HEATHCOTT AND VERIBEST FALCONS FOOTBALL PHOTOS *Courtesy Amanda Heathcott, San Angelo, ca. 1997*

45 THREE PLAYERS FROM HOPEWELL, TX
Courtesy Prairie View Interscholastic League Coaches Association, Austin, ca. 1930s

43

45

44

46 GAME POSTER WACO HIGH VS. BRYAN HIGH AT WACO STADIUM *Courtesy Texas High School Football Hall of Fame, Waco, October 30, 1936*

47 MISSION EAGLES FOOTBALL SCHEDULE *Courtesy Mission Historical Museum, Mission, ca. 1947*

48 DECEMBER CALENDAR OF THE LUBBOCK WESTERNERS *Courtesy Texas High School Football Hall of Fame, Waco, ca. 1952*

46

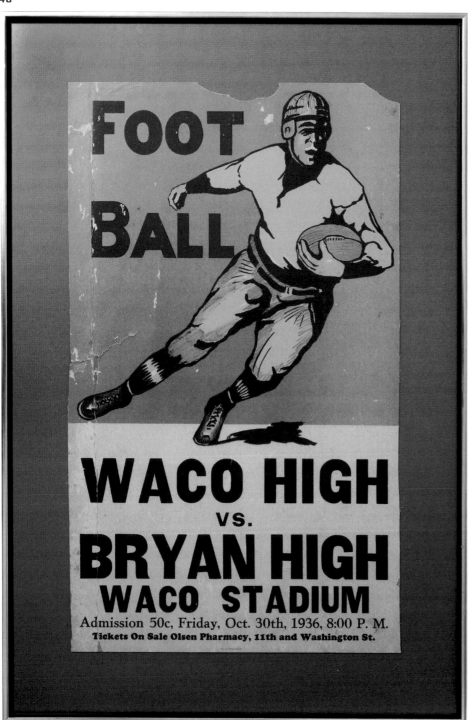

47

Mission Eagles
1947 FOOTBALL SCHEDULE

DATE	We	TEAMS	they		PLACE
SEPTEMBER 12	0	BROWNSVILLE	17	MARiVN	THERE
SEPTEMBER 19	7	EDINBURG	0	Fostone	THERE
SEPTEMBER 26		ST. JOSEPH ACADEMY		M	HERE
OCTOBER 3		DONNA			THERE
OCTOBER 10	26	MERCEDES	0	Bonnie	THERE
OCTOBER 17		RAYMONDVILLE			HERE
OCTOBER 24		OPEN			
OCTOBER 31	0	WESLACO	38	M	THERE
NOVEMBER 7		RIO GRANDE CITY			HERE
NOVEMBER 15	47	LA FERIA	10	Helen	HERE
NOVEMBER 21	19	PHARR–SAN JUAN–ALAMO	7	Helen	THERE

48

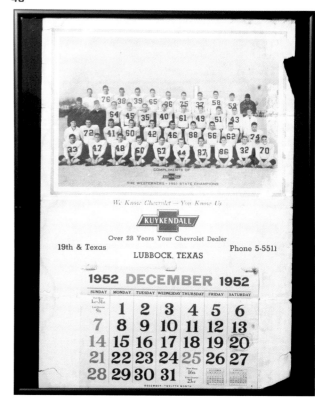

49 NIGHT FOOTBALL, LONDON HIGH SCHOOL FIELD, 8:00 P.M. *Courtesy New London Museum, ca. 1934*

50 MISSION EAGLES FOOTBALL PROGRAM *Courtesy Mission Historical Museum, Mission, ca. 1948*

51 BLACKWELL HORNETS FOOTBALL SCHEDULE *Courtesy Blackwell High School, ca. 1917*

52 AMARILLO SANDIES VS LUBBOCK WESTERNERS GAME PROGRAM *Courtesy Amarillo High School, November 11, 1943*

49

51

50

52

53 AMARILLO HS STATE CHAMPIONSHIP TROPHY *Courtesy Amarillo High School, ca. 1936*

UNIVERSITY INTERSCHOLASTIC LEAGUE
NORTH TEXAS CHAMPIONS
FOOTBALL
1920
TIED WITH HOUSTON HEIGHTS
FOR STATE HONORS

55 DAINGERFIELD TIGERS CHAMPIONSHIP RING *Courtesy Balfour, Austin, ca. 2010*

56 HENDERSON LIONS CHAMPIONSHIP RING *Courtesy Balfour, Austin, ca. 2010*

57 CIBOLO STEELE KNIGHTS CHAMPIONSHIP RING *Courtesy Balfour, Austin, ca. 2010*

58 RICHLAND SPRINGS COYOTES CHAMPIONSHIP RING *Courtesy Balfour, Austin, ca. 2010*

59 MART PANTHERS CHAMPIONSHIP RING *Courtesy Balfour, Austin, ca. 2010*

60 ABILENE EAGLES VS WACO TIGERS *Courtesy Abilene High School, December 22, 1922*

55

56

57

58

59

60

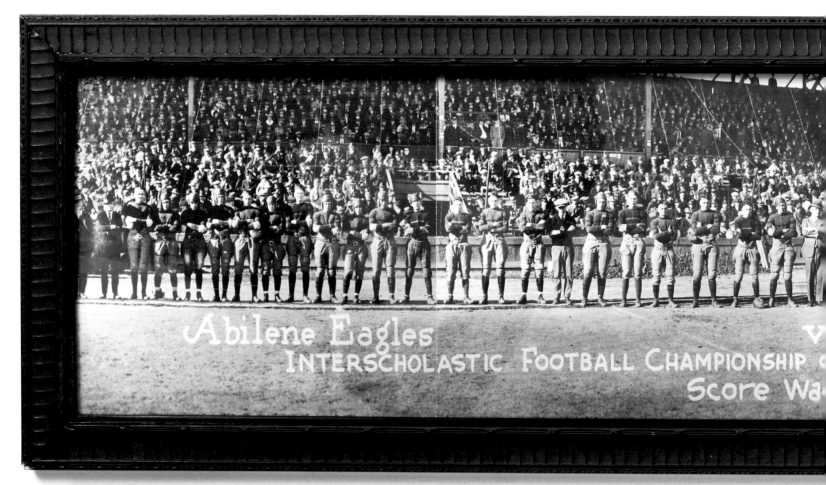

61 PEARLAND OILERS CHAMPIONSHIP RING *Courtesy Balfour, Austin, ca. 2010*

62 CARTHAGE BULL-DOGS CHAMPIONSHIP RING *Courtesy Balfour, Austin, ca. 2010*

63 ALEDO BEARCATS CHAMPIONSHIP RING *Courtesy Balfour, Austin, ca. 2010*

64 FALLS CITY BEAVERS CHAMPIONSHIP RING *Courtesy Balfour, Austin, ca. 2010*

65 IDALOU WILDCATS CHAMPIONSHIP RING *Courtesy Todd and Jim Morgan, Jostens - Top of Texas, ca. 2010*

66 BROWNSVILLE EAGLES CHAMPIONS WALLET *Courtesy Brownsville Independent School District, ca. 1962*

67 ABILENE HIGH EAGLES CHAMPION JERSEY *Courtesy Harold's Pit Bar-B-Que, Inc., Abilene, ca. 2009*

68 BLANCO PANTHERS STATE CHAMPS *Courtesy Blanco High School, ca. 2002*

66

67

68

69 HARROLD HS TEAM PHOTO *Courtesy Harrold High School, ca. 1938*

70 AUSTIN HS STATE CHAMPIONSHIP RING *Courtesy The Brian W. Schenk Archives at Austin High School, ca. 1942*

70

69

1938
DISTRICT CHAMPIONS

WELDON ROGERS
First Captain

LORENE (FRAZIER) WALSER
First Football Queen

BACK ROW
(Left to Right)
Supt. S. P. Vick, Ralph Houtchins, Jack Sampley, Carlton Huff, Newell Gladden, Donald Wetherbee, Sharon Haralson, Sonny Turpin, Coach T. B. Yarbrough

FRONT ROW
(Left to Right)
Ernest Standridge, LeRoy Hines, Captain Weldon Rogers, Pat Patterson, Preacher Huff, Boyd Vaughn, Eugene Hollis

HARROLD'S FIRST FOOTBALL TEAM

PRESENTED TO 1982 HARROLD HIGH SCHOOL STUDENT BODY BY SHERIL "PREACHER" HUFF, SENIOR CLASS AND STUDENT BODY PRESIDENT, 1939-1940

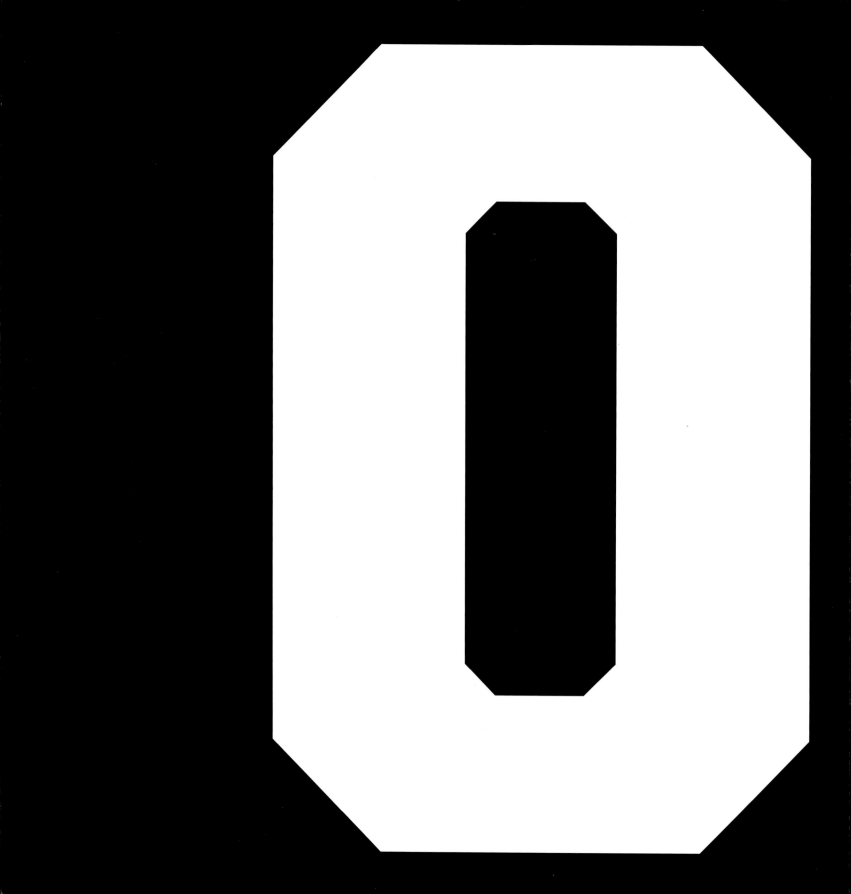

**71 SAN ANTONIO
JEFFERSON HS LASSOS
DRUM & BUGLE CORPS
MAJOR BATON** *Courtesy
Mary Eanes Brophy Garven,
ca. 1940*

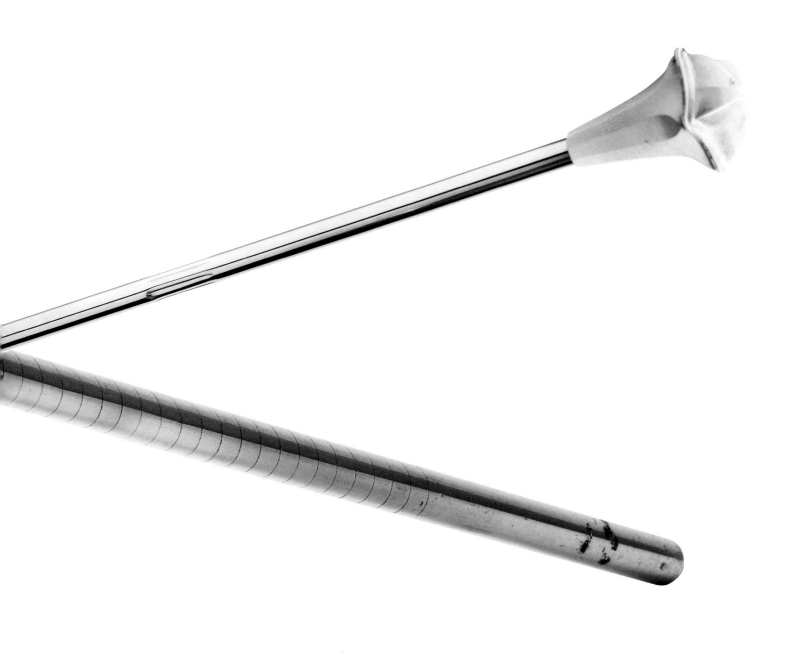

**73 MARY EANES
BROPHY GARVEN,
LASSOS MAJOR** *Courtesy
Mary Eanes Brophy Garven,
ca. 1940*

74

**74 SAN ANTONIO
JEFFERSON HS LASSOS
DRUM & BUGLE CORPS
UNIFORM** *Courtesy Betty
Towery Alkire, Class of 1944
(Lasso blouse, belt, and skirt);
Gloria Mabrito Williams, Lasso
Major, Class of 1944 (Lasso
rope); Phyllis Tennis Ramby,
Class of 1957 (Lasso hat); Joe-
Beth Kirkpatrick, Class of 1971
(Lasso scarf); Suzanne Olafson
Cude, Class of 1953 (Lasso
brown boots) ca. 1940s-50s*

**75 LASSOS
PERFORMING** *Courtsey
Gloria Mabrito Williams,
ca. 1944*

**76 LASSOS MEDALS
AND MERIT BARS**
*Courtesy Barbara Chambers
Touchstone, Class of 1959,
ca. 1957*

76

75

77 WILSON HS TWIRLER UNIFORM *Courtesy Tracy Ray Wancho, Cedar Park, ca. 1978*

78 EDINBURG HS SERGEANETTES CAPE *Courtesy Edinburg High School Sergeanettes Dance Team, ca. 1940s*

77

78

79

**80 PORT NECHES-
GROVES' INDIAN SPIRIT
SPEAR** *Courtesy Port
Neches-Groves High School,
ca. 1964-65*

81 STINNETT HS BAND UNIFORM *Courtesy Stinnett High School Ex-Students, ca. 1979*

82 HARLINGEN HS CONQUISTADOR BAND UNIFORM *Courtesy Harlingen Arts & Heritage Museum, ca. 1920s*

81

82

**83 WOODSON HS BAND
UNIFORM** *Courtesy
Woodson High School, Abilene,
ca. 1967*

83

84

85

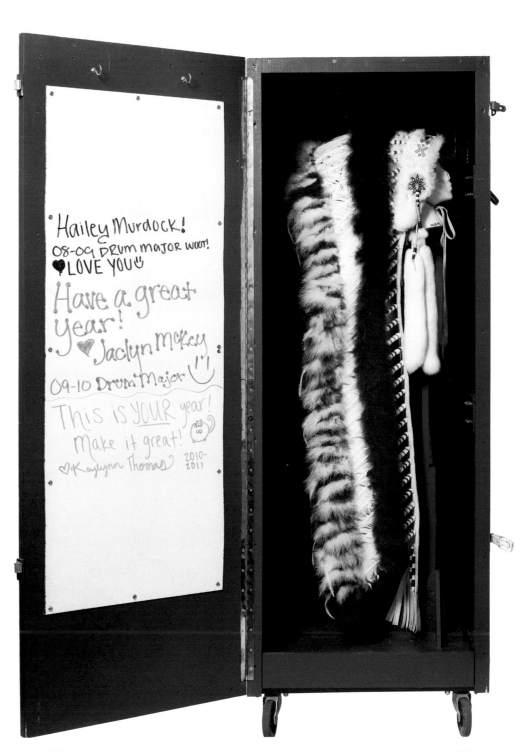

MORE THAN THE GAME   69

89 GREENVILLE HS FLAMING FLASHES UNIFORM *Courtesy Greenville High School*

90 PHILLIPS HS CHEERLEADER'S UNIFORM, MEGAPHONE, AND POM-POM *Courtesy Phillips High School*

91 TEXAS HS CHEERLEADER'S UNIFORM *Courtesy Texarkana Independent School District, ca. 2010*

89

90

91

**92 FORT WORTH
ARLINGTON HEIGHTS
HS CHEERLEADER
LETTER SWEATER**
*Courtesy Joe Nick Patoski, Fort
Worth Arlington Heights High
School, Class of 1969, ca. 1968*

92

93

94

95 PHOTOGRAPH OF
NORTHWEST HS
TEXANS MASCOT
© 2010 Bill Kennedy

96 PHOTOGRAPH OF
HOUSTON LUTHERAN
SOUTH PIONEERS
MASCOT © 2010 Bill Kennedy

97 PHOTOGRAPH OF
DEKALB HS BEARS
MASCOT © 2010 Bill Kennedy

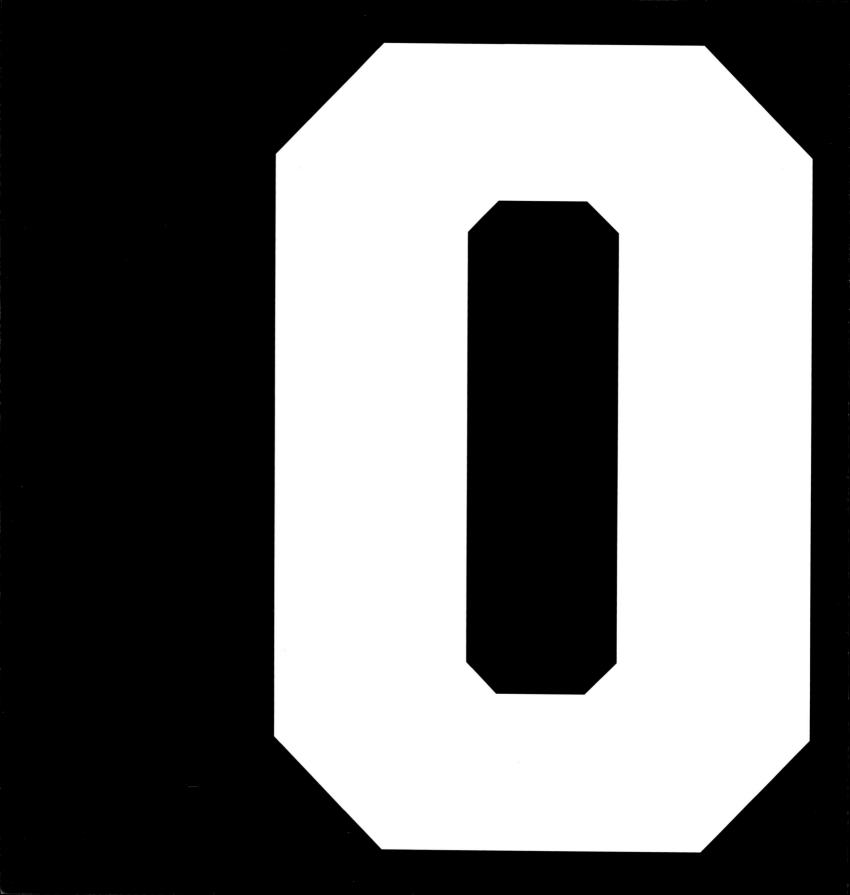

4

**99 ABILENE HS SINGLE
HOMECOMING MUM**
Courtesy Abilene High School

**100 ABILENE HS DOUBLE
HOMECOMING MUM**
Courtesy Abilene High School

99

100

101 STINNETT HS HOMECOMING GARTER *Courtesy Stinnett High School Ex-Students*

102 I. M. TERRELL, FORT WORTH HOMECOMING GAME PROGRAM *Courtesy Beverly J. Washington, Fort Worth, ca. 1949*

103 FORT WORTH NORTHSIDE HS CHEERLEADERS AND SPONSOR *Courtesy Billy W. Sills Center for Archives, Fort Worth Independent School District, ca. 1945*

101

102
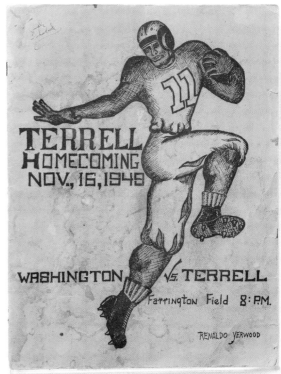

103

105 PEARLAND HS HOMECOMING SPIRIT RIBBON *Courtesy Anita Holmes, Pearland, ca. 1983*

106 ABILENE HS HOMECOMING SPIRIT RIBBON *Courtesy Abilene High School, ca. 1992*

107 BLACKWELL HS HOMECOMING QUEEN WEARING CAPE *Courtesy Blackwell School, Marfa, ca. 1957*

108 BLACKWELL HS HOMECOMING CAPE *Courtesy Blackwell School, Marfa, ca. 1957*

109 HOMECOMING DRESS *Courtesy Costumes By Dusty, Arlington, ca. 1950s*

110 TEXAS SCHOOL FOR THE DEAF HOMECOMING CROWN *Courtesy Heritage Center, Texas School for the Deaf Alumni Association, Austin, ca. 1967*

111 KATY TIGERS METAL ART *Courtesy Katy Bengal Brigade and Cheerleaders, Katy, ca. 2010*

112 MONAHANS HS SPIRIT RIBBON *Courtsey Marie Simmons Nabors, Monahans, ca. 1959*

**113 PHILLIPS HS
FOOTBALL SHAPED
COIN PURSE WITH
FOOTBALL SCHEDULE**
*Courtesy Phillips High School,
ca. 1971*

**114 SEASON TICKET
BOOKLET FOR BOOKER
T. WASHINGTON HS**
*Courtesy The H. J. Lutcher
Stark Center for Physical Cul-
ture & Sport, Austin, ca. 1949*

**115 "SUGAR LAND
EXPRESS" PAINTING
OF KEN HALL** *Courtesy Ken
and Gloria Hall, Fredericksburg*

113

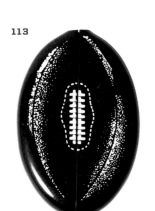

114

SECTION A
ROW 8
SEAT 7
LEOPARDS vs.
FORT WORTH
Oct. 13, 1949, 8:15 P. M.

— RESERVED SEAT —
Washington Leopards vs.
B. T. W. (Dallas)
LEOPARD STADIUM, Thurs., Nov. 3
Conference Game
Reserved Seat $1.00—Tax Included
8:15 P. M.

115

116 DONNA HS RED-SKINS SPIRIT RIBBON *Courtesy Richard Avila and Luz Padriza, ca. 1961*

117 SAN ANTONIO THOMAS JEFFERSON HS SPIRIT RIBBON *Courtesy Rica W. Kinnard, TJHS, Class of 1962, ca. 1961*

118 STINNETT HS SPIRIT RIBBON *Courtesy Stinnett High School Ex-Students*

119 ODESSA PERMIAN PANTHERS SPIRIT RIBBON *Courtesy Susan Thornton, Odessa, ca. 1973*

116

117

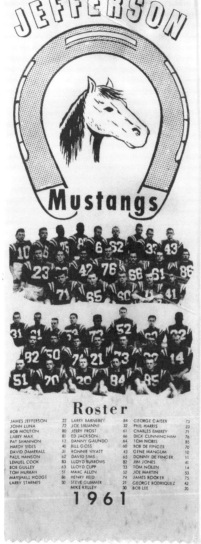

118

119

120 PORT ARTHUR HS FOOTBALL SHAPED PIGGY BANK *Courtesy Museum of the Gulf Coast, Port Arthur*

121 PHILLIPS BLACK-HAWKS FOOTBALL HELMET PIGGY BANK *Courtesy Phillips High School*

122 PHILLIPS BLACK-HAWKS LIGHTER *Courtesy Phillips High School,*

123 STINNETT HS RATTLERS ASHTRAY *Courtesy Stinnett High School Ex-Students, ca. 1968*

124 MONAHANS HS SPIRIT RIBBON *Courtesy Marie Simmons Nabors, ca. 1959*

128 STRIK'EM SNAKES STINNETT RATTLERS BOBBLE HEAD *Courtesy Stinnett High School Ex-Students, ca. 1968*

129 AUSTIN REAGAN HS FOOTBALL PLAYER FIGURINE *Courtesy Larry Miller, Austin, ca. 1970*

130 PHILLIPS BLACK-HAWKS BOBBLE HEAD *Courtesy Phillips High School, ca. 1955*

128

STRIK'EM SNAKES
STINNET RATTLERS

129

NATIONAL 1970 STATE

R

130

HAWKS

131 LITTLE SOUTH-WEST CONFERENCE DRINKING GLASS *Courtesy Texas High School Football Hall of Fame, Waco, ca. 1961-1967*

132 LINCOLN LA MARQUE EAGLES VS BAYTOWN CARVER PANTHERS GAME PRO-GRAM *Courtesy Prairie View Interscholastic League Coaches Association, Austin, ca. 1957*

133 MONAHANS HS SPIRIT TAG *Courtesy Marie Simmons Nabors, ca. 1957*

134 SOUTHLAKE CARROLL DRAGONS COWBELL *Courtesy Southlake Carroll Independent School District*

131

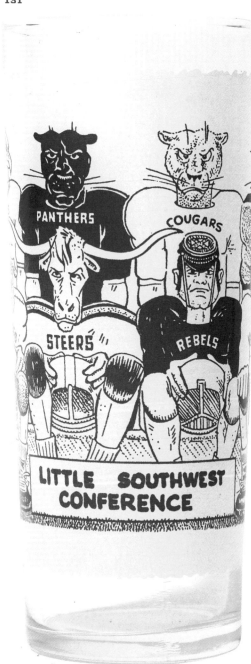

133

134

132

137 212° SIGN SUPPORTING CANADIAN HS *Courtesy Canadian High School, ca. 2010*

138 PERMIAN PANTHERS MOJO LICENSE PLATE COVER *Courtesy Susan Thornton, Odessa, ca. 1972*

139 GO HARD OR GO HOME YARD SIGN *Courtesy Joe Nick Patoski, Wimberley, ca. 2010*

140 REFUSE TO LOSE YARD SIGN *Courtesy Joe Nick Patoski, Wimberley, ca. 2010*

137

138

139

140

Masonic Home High School vs. Polytechnic High School *November 21, 1940, Courtesy Fort Worth Star–Telegram Collection, Special Collections, The University of Texas at Arlington Library*

LIST OF TIMELINE OBJECTS

01 BALL HIGH'S HAND-WRITTEN LINEUP FOR THE GAME *Courtesy Texas High School Football Hall of Fame, Waco, ca. 1892*

02 ORANGE HS FIRST FOOTBALL TEAM *Courtesy Heritage House Museum, Orange, October 15, 1909*

03 EL PASO FOOTBALL TEAM *Courtesy El Paso High School, ca. 1908*

04 1921 CLEBURNE CHAMPIONSHIP TEAM *Courtesy Cleburne High School, ca. 1920*

05 RAYMOND T. "PROF" BYNUM *Courtesy Abilene High School, ca. 1930s*

06 THOMAS JEFFERSON HS LASSOS IN WASHINGTON, DC *Courtesy Mary Eanes Brophy Garven, Class of 1940, San Antonio Jefferson Lassos, ca. 1939*

07 MIGHTY MITES COACH RUSTY RUSSELL *Courtesy Fort Worth Star–Telegram, Special Collections, The University of Texas at Arlington, August 11, 1936*

08 LONDON HS *Courtesy New London Museum, ca. 1932*

09 MISSION EAGLES FOOTBALL TEAM *Courtesy Mission Historical Museum, Mission, ca. 1939-40*

10 NORTH SIDE HS BAND *Courtesy Billy W. Sills Center for Archives, Fort Worth Independent School District, ca. 1945*

11 FRANKIE GROVES *Courtesy Hutchinson County Historical Museum, Borger, ca. 1947*

12 KEN HALL *Courtesy Texas High School Football Hall of Fame, Waco, ca. 1950s*

13 ABILENE HS CHAMPIONSHIP TEAM *Courtesy Abilene High School, ca. 1956*

14 EMORY BELLARD *Courtesy Texas High School Football Hall of Fame, Waco*

15 DONNA REDSKINS 2A STATE CHAMPIONS *Courtesy Richard Avila, ca. 1961*

16 COACHING STAFF AT CARVER HS IN WACO *Courtesy Texas High School Football Hall of Fame, Waco, ca. 1964*

17 UWE VON SCHAMANN EASTERN HILLS HS *Fort Worth, Courtesy Uwe von Schamann, Edmond, Oklahoma, ca. 1975*

18 BIG SANDY STATE CHAMPIONSHIP TEAM *Courtesy Texas High School Football Hall of Fame, Waco, ca. 1975*

19 GORDON WOOD *Courtesy Texas High School Football Hall of Fame, Waco*

20 FRIDAY NIGHT LIGHTS: A TOWN, A TEAM, AND A DREAM BOOK *By H.G. Bissinger, Courtesy of Da Capo Press, 1990.*

21 G. A. MOORE AUTO-GRAPHED FOOTBALL TO GORDON WOOD *Courtesy Gordon Wood Hall of Champions Museum, Brownwood*

22 VERIBEST FALCONS "A. HEATHCOTT" YARD SIGN *Courtesy Amanda Heathcott, San Angelo, ca. 1997*

23 SEALY TIGERS, TITLE-TOWN, TEXAS SIGN *Courtesy Alan R. Konieczny, Sealy, ca. 1997*

24 RIDE FOR THE BRAND, MIDLAND LEE REBELS POSTER *Courtesy Texas High School Football Hall of Fame, Waco, ca. 1998-99*

25 G. A. MOORE *Courtesy Fred Helms, Celina*

26 SOUTHLAKE CARROLL DRAGONS WITH 2004 STATE CHAMPIONSHIP TROPHY *Courtesy Southlake Carroll Independent School District, ca. 2004*

27 2008 KATY HS CHAMPIONS, THE KATY TIMES, *Courtesy The Katy Times, December 24, 2008*

28 LAKE TRAVIS CAVALIERS CHAMPIONSHIP RING AND RING BOX *Courtesy Lake Travis High School, ca. 2010*

INSIDE BACK COVER
N. Third St. and Main
Stratford, Texas, ©2004 Bill Kennedy